PRAISE FOR *TEACHING IN THE DIGITAL AGE*

"Brian earns an A+ for providing educators with the tools and resources needed to transform conventional classrooms into modern spaces brimming with twenty-first-century digital practices. His creative, practical, personal approach makes it easy to update even the most traditional classroom. *Teaching in the Digital Age* personally motivated me to forge ahead with these new and effective practices. This book is an entertaining and educational journey for any teacher who strives to be a lifelong learner and wants to develop a relationship with his/her students academically, emotionally, and technologically."
　　—Renee Wilberg, Kindergarten Teacher

"This book has something for everyone—from the technophobe to the technocrat. Teachers can start where they feel comfortable and proceed step-by-step through the technology activities. A must-read resource!"
　　—Bonnie K. Roelle, Director, Office of Early Childhood Programs, Chicago
　　　Public Schools

"Brian paints an inspirational picture for the future of early childhood learning, seamlessly and playfully blending digital tools into the classroom and helping educators of all experience levels empower their students to create and share ideas."
　　—Andy Russell, Co-Founder, Launchpad Toys

"A terrific, path-breaking resource, chock-full of practical advice for early educators who are transforming their classrooms for a digital age."
　　—Michael Levine, Executive Director, Joan Ganz Cooney Center,
　　　Sesame Workshop

"Every day, teachers consider students' needs and set learning goals, and then choose the best tools—water or sand, crayons or paints, words or images. Brian Puerling lays out a realistic yet innovative framework for integrating technology among those tools—clear-eyed about not only the when, where, and how, but most importantly the why. I predict well-worn and marked-up copies of *Teaching in the Digital Age* in early learning centers, elementary classrooms, and Ed schools."

—David W. Kleeman, President, American Center for Children and Media

"I know firsthand how Brian Puerling's insightfulness and creativity enhanced my children's learning and inspired them for future growth. *Teaching in the Digital Age* provides a roadmap on how to use technology in the classroom for teachers and parents alike, which can lead to a fun, exciting, and personal educational experience for impressionable young minds. This book demonstrates the value of allowing creativity and exploration to exist in both school and home."

—Jonathan Harris, parent

"Often our students are more comfortable with technology than we are as adults. In *Teaching in the Digital Age*, Brian Puerling takes the sometimes daunting idea of using technology in meaningful ways with young children and makes it look not just achievable for teachers, but something all students deserve. Brian skillfully mixes practical advice, thoughtful rationale, authentic classroom scenarios, the voices of experts and colleagues, and his own expertise to provide teachers with a vision for how technology can be used seamlessly in a classroom. Brian builds on children's natural interest in technology and combines it with effective instructional strategies to give you a vision for what high-quality learning can look like. You will learn more than just how to use technology to enhance learning. You will learn how to create engaging, high-quality learning environments and learning experiences for all children."

—Matt Glover, Educational Consultant and Author

"As someone who prepares initial early childhood educators, I have thought a lot about how to appropriately address the use of technology with young children. I even have to admit a bias related to its use, partly because of my own lack of skills and comfort level with technology, and largely because I did not know how to ensure that our undergraduate students learn to use technology with young children in an intentional and appropriate way.

Brian's book not only addressed my concerns, but also provided me with guidance and a wealth of ideas as to how to use various technologies to enhance learning for young children. There is a balance, but it was unfair of me to not consider the limitless potential that technology has for young children because I lacked the necessary knowledge. When reading Brian's book, it also occurred to me that in order to provide *all* children with the necessary prerequisite skills, comfort level, and ability to use technology in their future, we need to support them in using it in a meaningful and controlled way when they are in our care. Not all children will have access to the technology that can either level the playing field or cause further achievement gaps. Used in the appropriate ways that Brian describes, we can provide young children with one of the keys to future personal/social, academic and professional success. I am ready to 'embrace the uncertainty' and change the way I teach. The forms that Brian provided are particularly helpful in taking that first step in using technology to enhance learning in an appropriate way.

There is so much I could say about Brian's book. It is engaging, easy to follow, and, as the reader, I often felt that I was right there in the classroom as he was teaching. The scenes he describes bring to life the content and message of the book.

I remember when Brian traveled to Australia and was able to conduct some undergraduate research. When I reached chapter two, I had to smile at the reference to a content unit on Australia for four-year-olds brought to life through dramatic play and other centers. Brian brings his personal experiences to his teaching and then, with technology, is able to make the world an even smaller place. I also so appreciate that he is intent on using technology (photos, video clips, etc.) to dispel biases rather than perpetuate them."

—Barbara Gander, Early Childhood Education Faculty,
University of Wisconsin–La Crosse

Teaching in the Digital Age

TEACHING
IN THE
DIGITAL AGE

SMART TOOLS
for AGE 3 to GRADE 3

BRIAN PUERLING

Redleaf Press®
www.redleafpress.org
800-423-8309

Published by Redleaf Press
10 Yorkton Court
St. Paul, MN 55117
www.redleafpress.org

First edition 2012
Cover design by Jim Handrigan
Cover photograph © Michael Jung/Veer
Interior design by Jim Handrigan and typeset in Minion Pro
Printed in the United States of America
19 18 17 16 15 14 13 12   1 2 3 4 5 6 7 8

Image on page 56 courtesy of Shutterfly.
One More Story screenshots on page 100, © 2006 by One More Story Inc., are reprinted with permission. All rights reserved.
Photo-Sort screenshot on page 193, © 2010 by Romain Henry, is reprinted with permission. All rights reserved.
The Best Friends Book app screenshot on page 195, © 2008 by Todd Parr, is reprinted with permission. All rights reserved.
I Spy Riddle Race screenshot on page 197, © 2009 by Scholastic Entertainment Inc., is reprinted with permission. All rights reserved.
Toontastic: Story Arc Page screenshot on page 206, © 2011 by Launchpad Toys, is reprinted with permission. All rights reserved.

Library of Congress Cataloging-in-Publication Data
Puerling, Brian.
    Teaching in the digital age : smart tools for age 3 to grade 3 / Brian Puerling ; [foreword by] Carol Copple.
      p. cm.
    Summary: "Explore the many ways technology can enhance complete curriculum and assessment in the classroom. The book's strategies reflect Technology in Early Childhood Programs, the joint position statement of the National Association for the Education of Young Children and the Fred Rogers Center" — Provided by publisher.
    Includes bibliographical references and index.
    ISBN 978-1-60554-118-1 (pbk.)
    1. Early childhood education—Computer-assisted instruction. 2. Educational technology—United States. 3. Early childhood education—Curricula—United States.   I. Title.
LB1139.35.C64P84 2012
371.330973—dc23

                        2011050043

Printed on acid-free paper

To my wife, Emily —

you inspire me to be the best that I can be.

Contents

Foreword

Early childhood educators, it must be said, have not always welcomed technology with open arms. Some have concerns about whether computers, video, and the like take away time that children would better spend in play and other active and social pursuits. They worry about the excessive screen time in children's lives today. And these are valid concerns. Some uses of technology are, to say the least, a waste of children's time. At worst, they can contribute to children getting the habit of defaulting to passive and empty entertainment to occupy their time. Early childhood educators and parents should continue to oppose such excessive and inappropriate use of technology.

But this is not the kind of technology use that this excellent book describes. Rather, Brian Puerling shows us many lively, engaging, social, and thought-provoking ways to use technology with young children. He has been busily engaging with teachers and children in classrooms, including his own, and gleaning ideas from many people who are doing innovative things in learning environments. He shares inspiring ideas about a range of tools, from digital cameras to iPads, videoconferencing to audiorecorders. But the book is not really about technology; it is about learning, creativity, and engagement. The author knows a great deal about what interests and challenges children and has given a great deal of thought and study to how technology can be a catalyst and tool in many learning enterprises.

Further, *Teaching in the Digital* Age brings us not only the author's expertise but also the perspectives of more than a dozen other respected thinkers in the field, through both text and video segments. One such expert is Bonnie Blagojevic, a leader in developmentally appropriate technology integration, who gives this view of the rich potential that technology has for young children:

> If we feel strongly about educational topics such as nature appreciation, play, language, diversity, and social-emotional development, let's consider how technology can support these priorities. Show children how to use nature webcams on the Internet to peek into an eagle's nest and watch

eagles raise their young, observing and discussing what eagles eat, where they live, and how that connects with their own lives. Or teach children to use digital cameras to photograph their block constructions, print, and post them together with their stories and reflect with others about their creations. Collaborate by video chat with children and classrooms in other parts of the country or world and/or use "video visiting" to involve distant family members with classroom projects. Use technology to enrich, not replace, hands-on learning experiences so important to young children. (p. 18)

The book is full of valuable ideas from Brian and colleagues around the country who are developing and refining classroom uses of technology. And it seems to me that the early childhood field is launched upon a new phase in its approach to technology. One milestone of this is the recent publication of the National Association for the Education of Young Children (NAEYC)'s position statement on technology, developed with the Fred Rogers Center (FRC), which states both the cautions and the myriad opportunities for learning in technology and interactive media, as expressed here: "Thanks to a rich body of research, we know much about how young children grow, learn, play, and develop. There has never been a more important time to apply principles of development and learning when considering the use of cutting-edge technologies and new media" (NAEYC and FRC 2012, 1).

Like this position statement, *Teaching in the Digital Age* is grounded in a strong understanding of how children develop and learn, as well as in a great respect for teachers. Recognizing that it is teachers and families who know best the children they care for and teach, Brian encourages early childhood educators to make use of technology in their own ways suited to their own context. For example, in a program with families that have parents in the military or working difficult hours, and are thus unable to attend teacher conferences, a fresh possibility is videoconferencing. Not only can teacher and parents see one another, but the teacher can share the child's work samples, photographs of classroom learning, and other items that make the long-distance parent-teacher conference experience almost as real as meeting in person.

In encounters with technology, the reaction of many adults is, well, fear. Believe me, I identify deeply with technology anxiety. Yet even I—light years from being a comfortable-with-technology twenty-something—do not find this book intimidating. It is really quite reassuring and friendly, making the use of each tool accessible. Brian Puerling wisely encourages us to start small, beginning with just one new thing we would like to try. And many of his teaching ideas are far from high tech, using familiar items like digital cameras or audio-recorders but in new ways that are well within the comfort zone of the average early educator.

For all the reasons I have detailed, I am pleased to contribute this foreword and to enthusiastically commend this gem of a book to my fellow early childhood educators. I believe you will enjoy the adventures in teaching and learning that it welcomes you to embark on!

Carol Copple, PhD
Early Education Consultant

Acknowledgments

This book would not have been possible without the help and support of so many wonderful people in my undergraduate years at the University of Wisconsin–La Crosse. I want to thank Barb Gander for showing me how to critically reflect on my practice and dispositions. The children, staff, and families at the Campus Child Center showed me what a high-quality early childhood program community should look like.

I want to acknowledge the incredible faculty, staff, and families of Burley School in Chicago, Illinois. In my four years there, I always felt at home and comfortable trying something new. Thank you to Principal Barbara Kent for challenging me to experiment and try new things in my classroom. I want to extend a deep thanks to Kari Calabresa and Kristin Ziemke-Fastabend for being there when I felt stuck. Their words of encouragement truly kept me moving through this process.

The Chicago Public Schools Office of Early Childhood Education administrative staff—Debby Jobst, Chris Rosean, Bonnie Roelle, and Beatrice Colon—trusted me as I explored new and innovative practices in the classroom.

The amazing faculty, staff, and families at the Catherine Cook School in Chicago provide a learning environment where administrators, teachers, children, and families feel welcome to explore, discover, and reflect upon the many ways children can learn and develop. Thank you for helping readers see how strategies can be carried out through the provided videos in this book.

I am indebted to my friend Gail Conway of the Chicago Metro AEYC for being an amazing mentor and guide through navigating the many arenas of early childhood education.

I am especially grateful for the hard work and best practices of those professionals who contributed to this book: Andy Russell, Bonnie Blagojevic, David Kleeman, Meghan Residori, Maria Larios, Sheri Burkeen, David Curry, Cora Boucher, Kira Hamann, Nick Manesis, Sarah Stagmeier, Andrew Beights, Lauren Cohen, Barbra Fisher, Diane Salk, Ashley Wales, Beth Lambert,

Sharon Godley, Christine Caro Bowie, Jean Robbins, Pam Pifer, Carli McKenney, Mike Kruse, Kate Herron, Karla Beard-Leroy, Natalie Ripley, Rachel Kennedy, and Jennifer Berg-Wallish.

To Erin Stanfill, I want to extend a special thanks for her constant encouragement and support not only while I was writing this book but as we pursued our master's degrees at the Erikson Institute and our National Board Teacher Certification.

Kudos to the staff at the Erikson Institute for providing a high-quality graduate program from which I was able to develop a deep understanding of the many factors that influence how children grow and develop.

I want to thank the wonderful team at Redleaf Press. I truly appreciate their collaborative process of working with authors. Kyra Ostendorf, my editor, deserves special recognition for helping craft this resource for teachers.

Many thanks go to Chip Donohue for not only his contribution to this book but his contribution to the field of early childhood and his unending advocacy for meaningful technology use in classrooms and programs across the country.

I want to thank my family for their constant encouragement to embrace new challenges. To my wife, Emily: without your unending support, flexibility, and understanding, I could not have completed this book.

Introduction

On August 3, 2010, my wife and I hauled two enormous suitcases onto the Blue Line subway train headed for O'Hare International Airport. After we hustled our heavy bags into seats, I checked to make sure we had our tickets, and then I took a moment to catch my breath. As I did so, I could not help but notice the three consecutive rows of people reading from e-readers. Ironically, as I sat at Starbucks writing this introduction, I was interrupted by a woman who held out her iPad and asked if I could help her buy and download an e-book. Together we navigated the online store to get her set up. Immediately after this conversation, a man and his daughter next to me opened a laptop and began video chatting with an individual. Moments like these remind me of how technology has become woven into our everyday lives. The ways in which we gather and share information—in our personal lives and in teaching—has changed in remarkable ways in the past fifteen years. When I began teaching, I knew that technology could be used as an amazing tool to support children's growth and development. I began exploring the possibilities by thinking outside the box and simply experimenting with various technologies. The results were exciting and motivating.

Why This Book Is Needed

A recent report from the Joan Ganz Cooney Center at Sesame Workshop calls for the development of high-quality resources to support teachers in implementing technology in thoughtful, intentional ways in classrooms (Barron et al. 2011). Meanwhile, the National Association for the Education of Young Children and the Fred Rogers Center (2012) have also recently released their position statement on developmentally appropriate technology use in early childhood programs for children from birth to age eight. The position statement thoughtfully highlights important elements for practitioners to consider when implementing technology. Teachers need to consider how they select, use, and integrate technology with the nontechnological tools they are already using. They also need to consider how they will evaluate strategies in terms of effectiveness. The statement includes recommended guidelines for the implementation of particular strategies for given ages and development levels. This book is designed to address the components of the NAEYC and FRC position statement and also respect the wide-ranging skills that teachers possess. My hope is that it provides teachers with a set of tools to engage children with technology to support learning.

In classrooms, teachers and children can embrace new technologies to enhance the way they gather, share, analyze, create, apply, and assess information. The technologies available can be used in a whole host of ways that open doors to a multitude of possibilities. A digital voice recorder used by doctors and FBI agents to record conclusions and next steps can also be used by teachers to record conversations between children. An iPad, used at home to organize to-do and shopping lists, can be used in a classroom to quickly gather anecdotal notes on children in a class to be immediately sent to grade-level team members or other professionals. Technologies of our world are evolving at an astonishing rate. When Steve Jobs passed away in the fall of 2011, many were shocked and wondered what would happen to the pace of our technology development. The glass entrances of Apple stores across the country became tiled in notes by people thanking Mr. Jobs for his brilliance and for what

Brian Puerling and Chip Donohue of the Erikson Institute discuss common questions about and opportunities with today's technologies. (*www.redleafpress.org/tech/n-1.aspx*)

he brought to our world. Steve Jobs blazed a trail with his innovation in technology. People began to ask, "What will happen now that he's gone?" even as the development of new technologies continued to move full-speed ahead. Fortunately, the teams at Apple and elsewhere carry enough innovation and brilliance to keep up with the pace. Their strategies and ideas do not cease to amaze us as they move forward, releasing new and innovative technologies that continue to change the ways we live our daily lives and engage children with concepts.

Teachers need to know how to use new—and old—technology effectively and appropriately in classrooms. My hope is that this book is your go-to resource for using today's technology in your classroom.

Brian Puerling and Gail Conway of Chicago Metro AEYC discuss the information and opportunities that technology provides children and the need for training and professional development to support educators. (*www.redleafpress.org/tech/n-2.aspx*)

How to Use This Book

This book contains nine chapters, seven of which highlight a particular technology. Chapter 1 discusses challenges teachers face in utilizing new technologies in classrooms. It also provides messages from experts in the field of early childhood education about technology's role in young children's experiences. It explores how teachers can thoughtfully map their curriculum over the course of a year. Chapter 1 also identifies the importance of goal setting and how to thoughtfully do so.

Chapters 2 through 8 describe the following seven technologies and how they can be used in classrooms:

- cameras, chapter 2
- projectors and document cameras, chapter 3
- audio recordings, chapter 4
- videoconferencing and webcams, chapter 5
- publication and presentation tools, chapter 6
- videos, chapter 7
- multi-touch mobile devices, chapter 8

Considering the multitude of ways in which these technologies can be used, each chapter is broken down into three sections. These sections are intended to help teachers understand how a particular technology can be used to:

1. Support learning.

2. Assess student knowledge and teacher practice.

3. Exhibit learning.

Each chapter also includes forms you can use that encourage reflection on and evaluation of strategies used in your classroom. I also utilize a technology throughout the book for easy access to videos and forms: QR (quick reference) codes provide you with an opportunity to view video clips for a deeper look into these practices. The videos are intended to help you develop a firm understanding of the ideas and practices described throughout the book. Access the videos by scanning the QR code with your smartphone or iPad, using a quick reference application. If you don't have easy access to this technology, you can find the same video online at the URL listed next to each QR code. Similarly, the forms at the end of each chapter also have QR codes. You can scan the QR codes using a QR code-scanning application on a multi-touch mobile device and instantly have the form ready for use. These forms can be imported into many of the applications described throughout the chapters. If you are unable to scan the codes, permission is granted on each form to photocopy it, or you can access the forms electronically by following the URL address next to each QR code.

The Toolbox Tips in the book are specific to each chapter's technology. The tips include questions that I recommend you consider when moving forward with particular strategies or acquiring certain equipment. The overall goal of the Toolbox Tips is to help you evaluate your unique situation and move forward toward new strategies in a way that best suits your circumstances.

THE STRATEGIES

The strategies described in the book have been carried out by teachers just like you. The anecdotes and examples of actual learning experiences are from my classroom or from friends' and colleagues' classrooms. Though specific examples are provided, I am not suggesting that you replicate them in your classroom. I see the strategies as seeds. Each seed, no matter where it is planted, will grow differently depending on the environment and what resources it has. While the settings and age groups may not be exactly like yours, I do hope that you can connect with and be inspired by what you read. Know that you shouldn't expect to exactly replicate a strategy in the book. The strategies are here to inspire you—make them your own by connecting them to the children you work with and the technology that is available to you. It is important for you to be cognizant of the resources available to you and your students' abilities and background experiences so that these strategies are implemented in ways that best meet the needs of each unique group of children.

Some of the technology presented in this book may be new to you. Or the capabilities and operations may be unfamiliar. Because much of today's technology is new, teachers can easily become overwhelmed and unmotivated. I have worked with educators from various programs, and several have said, "Brian, there are so many things I want to try, but I don't know where to start. What do I do?" If this is how you feel, I recommend you identify one strategy in this book and try it in your classroom. Choosing the strategy will be a different process for each individual. To help you begin thinking about where to start, I suggest that while reading, you think about these important factors to determine which strategy to select:

- age of children,

- developmental level of children,

- each family's technological competencies,

- your own technological competencies,

- resources/equipment present in the classroom or throughout school,

- security of equipment,

- curriculum goals,

- administrative support,

- potential collaborative partners, and

- technology that children will engage with in future grades.

It may helpful to jot down some notes while reflecting on these factors. After doing so, tuck the notes in the back in chapter 9, where later they can be used to help in planning and implementing new strategies. Chapter 9 not only identifies strategies and frameworks to help with planning and implementation; it also provides various strategies to encourage reflection on the effectiveness of particular activities or experiences. This chapter also acknowledges challenges that arise when acquiring technology and attempts to ease anxieties through suggestions by and anecdotes about educators in difficult situations. You know that each child comes to class with his or her own set of skills that have been influenced by prior experiences. Similarly, each reader has his or her own unique set of skills in terms of technological competencies. Some readers will know how to operate both an iPad and a laptop, while others may only know how to operate a digital camera. It is my hope that you can easily identify the chapter and section that best address your needs and interests. In order to fully access what this book has to offer, I recommend reading chapter 1 to identify key elements to be aware of while reading through the strategies housed in chapters 2–8. In order to help employ new ideas and strategies, please read chapter 9 last. This chapter will help you identify how to carry out goals through collaboration, reflection, and revisiting curriculum mapping.

MEDIA CONSENT

Many of the strategies provided in this book direct teachers to take photographs and videos of children. In several cases, these strategies include ways to share the photographs and videos with others. Before you share photographs or videos of children, consult with your administrator to ensure that all necessary media consent forms are on file for the children. If consent forms are not on file, ask your administrator to provide one for you to have families sign. Explain to families how you plan to use photographs and videos. Be sure to include how you may use them to share how and what children have learned. The administration should keep signed consent forms on file each year from participating families.

◆　　◆　　◆

I have seen children embrace concepts I never thought possible. I have been impressed by the levels of thinking and speaking that young children are able to reach. I have seen how technology can be the escalator to higher-level teaching and learning. I encourage you to read this book with an open mind, a mind that is open to possibilities and new experiences for yourself and the children you teach. No doubt the strategies in this book will push some of you out of your comfort zone. I encourage you to think about teaching in a new way and try something you have never tried before. Ellin Oliver Keene (2008) titled one of the chapters in her book *To Understand* "To Savor the Struggle." She speaks about the value in being mystified by uncertainty. In the context of this book, there may be moments when you choose something to try that renders you nervous and unsure about what may come of it. It is important to remember that uncertainty is not negative. Embrace the uncertainty and look forward to what you and your students can learn. Like children learning about cause and effect in a water table, you need to explore today's technology to learn the possibilities. Good luck!

1
The Digital Classroom

www.redleafpress.org/tech/1-1.aspx

Elle, five years old, ran up to me with a picture she drew. She eagerly told me, "This girl is saying, 'I think the iPad is doing a good job helping us learn about digital books and the other applications.' The other person has an ELMO and says it's doing a good job with sharing books." As Elle talked, Kendall, also five years old, took interest in her work. He announced he wanted to write and draw about the iPad as well. He went to work and later brought me his picture, saying, "The iPad helps us read our books that we write." If you only observed my classroom for the half hour when these events occurred, you would know at least two things. First, both children are aware of technology utilized in the classroom. Second, and perhaps more important, they are developing an awareness of how the technology is helping their learning. Technology, whether it be an iPhone or an iPad, is changing the way we live our lives and interact with the world. And it's also changing the way we teach.

When a child sets foot in a classroom, she brings her entire life experience with her. She has learned how family members communicate, whether it be a big hug or a high five. She has learned a set of roles for family members, whether that means that dad is the person who cuts the grass or that mom is the person who does the laundry. She also may have learned what it means to be a sister, such as pitching in when a younger sibling needs help. She may have learned that each family member has his or her own belongings. Just as her interactions with and observations of family members shape her worldview, so do her interactions with technology. She may have observed family members using digital cameras to take photos, or perhaps she has seen family members using phones to play games. She also may have seen computers used to communicate and to listen to music. It is through experiences such as these that children implicitly learn possible roles for technology, general operation strategies, and general troubleshooting strategies (Plowman, McPake, and Stephen 2008). Young children are growing up in a wireless world. Many young children are used to parents taking photographs with their cell phones and then uploading them to a social media site with the push of a button. The ways in which people communicate and create are different than even ten years ago.

Young children today are growing up in an era similar to that of those who were born in the late 1950s and early 1960s, when the television swept through homes across the United States. My father, who was born in 1960, talks about his parents' loud rants about what it used to be like before television. He says they fervently described what it was like only to be able to listen to shows on the radio. They talked about how he and his siblings could never appreciate the television enough because they had not lived in an age without it. Today children hear similar stories about new devices such as digital voice recorders (DVRs), disposable cameras, and flip phones. Children today are not growing up with the loud crackling sound of a dial-up Internet connection. In dramatic play, I have seen children imitate adults talking on cell phones by holding their palm to their ear.

As technology continues to transform daily life worldwide, teachers need to prepare children for the technology skills they will need as they participate in society. Teachers who thoughtfully show children how to use various forms of technology to enrich their learning and lives have classrooms where children can go online with a teacher to buy a book, present knowledge through the creation of videos and podcasts, use their creativity to write their own digital books, and bring inanimate objects to life through animation in an iPad application (Mitchell 2007). Technology is one more tool teachers can use to support lifelong learning.

It is important to hold ongoing conversations about the developmentally appropriate use of technologies with families, team members, and assistants. The more your professional community and partners understand your vision and intention, the more your support system expands. No matter where you are, there is a way to obtain technology for your classroom or setting. Families can be invited to donate their used iPods and iPhones to classrooms rather than recycling centers. When donated equipment is not a possibility, grant programs may be a solution. A few useful grant programs are described in chapter 9.

Dr. Jean Robbins and Dr. Pam Pifer, the Early Childhood and Lower School Division Heads of the Catherine Cook School, discuss technology in the lives of young children. (*www.redleafpress.org/tech/1-2.aspx*)

My friend and colleague Chip Donohue, PhD, director of distance learning at the Erikson Institute and senior fellow at the Fred Rogers Center for Early Learning and Children's Media at Saint Vincent College, has been an instrumental figure in organizing how technology is used in early childhood settings. Before you begin to explore the strategies in this book, Chip has some words of encouragement for you.

It is clear that the digital age is upon us. Technology and digital media are deeply integrated into the personal and professional lives of early childhood teachers and in the home lives of the young children, parents, and families they work with. In a world in which technology use is ubiquitous and the tools are woven into the fabric of our environment and culture, early childhood educators need to be digitally literate (technology and media). It's essential that educators can make informed and appropriate decisions about whether, when, and how to use technology with young children, and how to support parents and families as they wrestle with choices related to screen time, access to digital media, and technology use.

To be effective and empowered decision makers, early childhood educators need to become prepared for their critical role in integrating technology into early childhood settings and mediating its use and impact. They need opportunities to learn about effective, appropriate, and intentional use of technology in teacher-preparation and professional development programs. In addition, making informed choices about online degree programs and professional development opportunities and having the technology skills to be a successful online learner are fast becoming essential tools for working early childhood professionals. We don't have a choice. The digital age is here—analog thinking and teaching methods won't support the opportunities for teaching, learning, communicating, collaborating, and creating with digital technology and media.

Early childhood educators, parents, and families need guidance to make informed decisions about how to support learning through technology, what technology tools and screen media are appropriate, when to integrate technology into an early childhood setting and at home, and how to use technology to enhance communication. Educators also need to know how to support the digital literacy of parents and children.

Some worry that technology is getting in the way of relationships, communication, and community; but where some see threats, I see opportunities. I think the digital age offers new opportunities for early childhood educators to build stronger relationships, support parents and families in new ways, and empower them to be confident and effective technology mediators at home by sharing knowledge about how positive uses of technology can support children's learning and development. I'm also very excited about opportunities for co-viewing and co-media engagement that many digital tools and media offer and encourage. We can use technology as a tool to connect us and to bring adults and children back together rather than to force them apart.

What I can say with confidence is that technology tools will keep getting faster, more powerful, and cheaper. My friend Warren Buckleitner (2011a), of *Children's Technology Review*, remarked recently, "Nobody will uninvent the iPad." It's time for early childhood educators to embrace these tools and to find ways to prepare young children for success in a digital age.

In my work as a senior fellow at the Fred Rogers Center, I have had the opportunity to learn about how Fred mastered the technology of his day—television—and turned it into an amazing tool for supporting the social and emotional development of young children and providing affirmation, support, and encouragement for parents. Fred said, "I went into television because I hated it so, and I thought there was some way of using this fabulous instrument to be of nurture to those who would watch and listen" (Millman 1999). That's our challenge in the digital age: turning these tools into fabulous instruments that support young children, parents, families, and educators. I don't think we need an app for that. We just need to start playing with the tools and figuring how best to use them, and to think about how our smartphones and tablet computers are already fabulous instruments. As my friends in New Zealand say, "Have a play."

Chip makes some extremely important points in his message to us practitioners. He directs teachers to become educated in new technologies. We need to know how new (and old) technologies can be used in our daily lives to learn, create, and communicate. It is important that teachers know how today's technology and digital media can be used before teaching with them. Chip ends his piece with "Have a play." As early childhood educators, we advocate for the best practice of playing to learn in classrooms. As adults, we, too, can play to learn—and with technology, playing has never been more fun. I remember meeting with friends and colleagues for the first time in a Google+ video chat room. The six of us were playing with the new technology, educating ourselves and pushing the boundaries of the new program. Naturally, as we played and learned, we began discussing the possibilities of how it could facilitate learning and communication in all sorts of contexts. Play is an important part of our entire lives.

A study done by Lori Takeuchi (2007) at the Joan Ganz Cooney Center at Sesame Workshop concluded with several recommendations for the industry of technology and young children. One recommendation was that new and innovative technology be developmentally appropriate, offering opportunities for children to take in new information, create, share, communicate, cooperate, and coordinate with others. While writing this book and narrowing down strategies that meet these recommendations, I began communicating with Andy Russell. Andy is a brilliant individual who cofounded Launchpad Toys and today is developing high-quality iPad applications for young children. In my conversations with him, I learned about his thoughtfulness in the development of his digital experiences for children. He described how digital play is woven within all experiences he develops. Andy learned about the value of play at a young age and decided early on that he was going to develop exciting educational toys for children. Here's his story.

I started playing with Legos at around age three, and I've never really stopped. My collection began with a modest number of space vehicles, grew to a galactic empire, detoured briefly with a few open-sea adventures on a barbarous pirate ship, and then finally got serious with a model town. And by "serious" I mean that my parents had to renovate our basement to carve out enough space for our small plastic city.

My Lego collection was not just a toy or a hobby; it ran much deeper for me. On one level, it was a laboratory. Of course, I always started with the standard instructions, but with very few exceptions those predefined models were quickly disassembled and fashioned into various contraptions, valued more for their unique pieces than for Lego's original design. I could build and model to my imagination's (fairly infinite) content without concern—unlike my father's woodshop or the chemistry set that collected dust in the closet. On another level, my Lego collection was a puppet theater, but one that constantly evolved and adapted to story lines and the desires of my imaginary characters. If Frankie Danger wanted to go bungee jumping, well, it was only a matter of time before a bungee tower was constructed right there in town. Finally, Legos were a social tool for me. My brother and I are four years apart with very different interests, but we shared a love for building that brought us together. I like to think of it as the kids' version of golf: you're engaged for hours, focused on the primary task, but not so focused that you can't work through a business deal or two (or in our case, a baseball card trade).

Ultimately, however, Legos were an inspiration for me as a designer. After seeing the movie *Big*, I decided at the wise old age of eight that I wanted to make toys when I grew up, and many years later, here I am, pretty much living the Josh Baskin/Tom Hanks life (minus the giant trampoline and the fetish for baby corn). It wasn't just that I wanted to make Legos, which I did and still do; it was that Legos fell just a tad short of my dreams and expectations. When I play with toys, and I think this is true for most kids, I create cartoons in my head. There are sets and props, characters, dialogue, animation, and . . . well, lots of explosions. It's like storytelling, but, sadly, without the telling part. Legos got me 95 percent there. I built fantastic sets, scripted complex story lines, and acted out great stories, but when it was time to head to bed, that story was gone and no one was the wiser for it. It killed me that I couldn't capture what I had created, that I couldn't share what I had imagined with friends or family. So, twenty years later, after stints in both the toy and video game industries, I cofounded a start-up in San Francisco called Launchpad Toys, where we're doing our best to create "Digital Legos"—not actually electronic bricks (though those are cool, too), but tools that allow kids to create and *share* their own stories at home, at school, and around the world.

We call Launchpad Toys a "Digital Play" company because mobile touch-screen devices like the iPad have the potential to blend all the kinesthetic, tangible, social, and mobile affordances of toys with the interactivity of gaming: an ideal platform for open-ended creative play. This enables us as designers to leap over traditionally entertainment-focused, linear, and achievement-oriented gaming conventions to create empowering, exploratory, and imaginative digital tools for kids to design and share their own ideas, stories, and drawings through play. It also enables us to move away from solitary "interactive adventures" to create collaborative tools for intergenerational play—to integrate, instead of exclude, the child's greatest mentor and advocate: family. By situating play in family spaces as opposed to the "computer room," we enable parents to join in while they cook dinner or clean up the house and, in turn, invite friends, siblings, grandparents, and cousins to step in as mentors, tutors, collaborators, and playmates. Rather than replacing parents and teachers with software, we can provide complementary tools enabling them to become facilitators and coaches rather than disciplinarians or test administrators.

Play is a natural learning environment. It's creative, experimental, and exploratory. Play is a crash course in problem solving and allows us to walk in the shoes of others to understand empathy, culture, and perspective. By designing toys and tools that spark the imagination, I hope to someday look back and see that Launchpad Toys has done for others what Lego has done for me: inspire creativity at play.

Andy's vision for technology infuses the need to play with the recommendations made by Takeuchi. Andy works to develop fun experiences for children that simultaneously invite knowledge, learning, collaboration, imagination, and creativity. Just as teachers work to include these elements in nontechnology-related learning experiences, it is also important to remember these elements when planning and implementing technology-related activities.

Technology is a significant gear in the machine that moves us through our daily lives. Though this is true, early childhood settings have not taken to what technology can offer a classroom community: learning, collaboration, and inquiry (Parette, Quesenberry, and Blum 2010). Never before has inquiry been supported to such an extent—children can access knowledge and information almost anywhere (Shuler 2009). The technology available today is designed so young children can participate and engage with the same devices that adults use.

Goal Setting

For teachers to embrace new ideas that will change the way they look at teaching and learning, it is important to carefully plan the route to change. Goals allow teachers to break down the task of change into smaller, doable components. If goals are not both manageable and measurable, teachers set themselves up for failure. I have spoken with many teachers who are interested in changing their practices, and I have asked them, "What is your goal? What do you want to try?" Several times I have heard responses such as "Well, I don't want to be afraid of the computer." Unfortunately, this goal is not manageable or measurable. In order for a teacher to overcome this fear, small goals must be established. If you have this fear, begin with a goal such as "I want to invite small groups of children to use the computer to create a newsletter." While reading this book, think about the curriculum you use, the materials you

have, and the skills necessary to carry out particular experiences. These points will help you identify particular strategies described in the book that may be an appropriate starting place for you. The strategies in this book may also help you develop brand-new ideas that you want to investigate. When goals are broken down, they are less intimidating and are more likely to be met. Use the Goal-Setting Sheet (form 1.1) to develop manageable and measurable goals.

Another goal might be "I am going to figure out a way to teach my students how to use the computers (or cameras or iPads) in my classroom." With this goal in mind, a teacher can use the Planning for Student Equipment Use Sheet (form 1.2) to record several other things, such as short- and long-term goals for technology use. The sheet encourages you to look at specific activity dynamics: Will children be working in pairs or small groups? Will they be watching videos? Will the printer be an option for them? In planning to meet certain

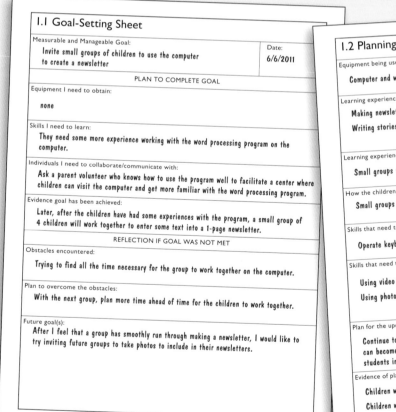

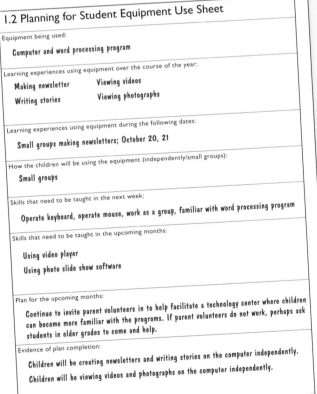

goals, it is important to remember other factors that may affect whether you meet your goal. For example, a teacher trying to encourage small groups to use a computer to create a newsletter will want to be sure that systems have been put in place to guide children to appropriate computer use. I recommend using both the Goal-Setting Sheet and the Planning for Student Equipment Use Sheet before starting to use a familiar technology in a new way or introducing a new technology. Using the forms together will ensure that your reflection and intention support the students and the experience in the best way possible.

CURRICULUM MAPPING: INFUSING TECHNOLOGY WITHIN

The NAEYC and FRC position statement on technology (2012) advocates that in high-quality early childhood programs, children should sing, talk, play outside, enjoy picture books, explore art materials, solve problems, ask questions, and make connections. However, it also indicates that children can seek an answer to a question by watching a video, create a video book on an iPad, and share their artwork or writing on a document camera. Technology is never to supplant; it is to supplement. Consider the examples on the following pages for how technology can fit into the other important experiences teachers provide children.

Mike Kruse, third-grade teacher, discusses the multitude of materials he uses to support his instruction, including an explanation of how he uses a document camera. (*www.redleafpress.org /tech/1-3.aspx*)

Grade Level: Preschool

ART

Paint at an easel

Experiment with shaving cream on a table

Create photo frames with various materials

Use an iPad drawing application to create digital artwork

PHYSICAL EDUCATION

Move body like familiar animals

Create necklaces with beads

Use an iPod Touch to capture video of children throwing and catching

Ride a tricycle

LANGUAGE

Sing songs

Learn greetings in other languages

Read poetry

Videoconference with a class in another region to explore accents

MATH

Sort items into groups

Draw simple shapes in sand

Use Montessorium applications to explore numbers and quantities up to ten

Dramatize cumulative stories

SCIENCE

Take a field trip to an aquarium or zoo

Collect leaves

Watch a video of applesauce being made before actually making it

Open up pumpkins

READING

Read stories daily

Dramatize stories with puppets

Project an e-book

Invite family members to be guest readers (physically or virtually)

HEALTH

Learn how to wash hands

Create signs with photos that show step-by-step how to put on a coat

Provide support in opening up one's own lunch containers

Ask for help when needed

MUSIC

Listen to music from various cultures

Invite professional musicians as visitors

Create a music center with instruments to explore

Record a class song to share on a class website

WRITING

Provide a choice of when to write

Provide a variety of materials to write with

Draw and write in pairs

Share writing/drawing using a document camera

SOCIAL STUDIES

Create a calming corner with cozy furniture

Read stories based on familiar childhood experiences

Conduct classroom meetings

Publish a (photo) book introducing staff and faculty at a school or in an early childhood setting

Grade Level: Kindergarten

ART

Explore textures of clay and paint

Draw simple shapes in a drawing application on a multi-touch mobile device

Identify colors in classroom

Match like colors on peers' clothing

PHYSICAL EDUCATION

Skip across a gymnasium

Use an iPad Reflex application to develop eye-hand coordination

Walk on a straight line

Participate in organized games as a whole group

LANGUAGE

Sing the alphabet

Sing songs related to phonemes

Identify rhyming words

Record conversations with children for e-portfolios

MATH

Create AB patterns with photographs of children in the classroom

Have experiences with puzzles

Observe environments to identify familiar shapes

Combine groups of manipulatives to create a new group

SCIENCE

Observe colors and textures of leaves under a document camera

Explore differences between lakes and rivers

Take a field trip to a nature center

Explore sinking and floating

READING

Enjoy a listening center with audiobooks read by classroom family members

Take home books to read

Read in small groups

Play word wall games

HEALTH

Sort foods into healthy and unhealthy groups

Take a field trip to a grocery store

Videotape family traditions for meal preparation at home

Sample new foods

MUSIC

Create instruments in an art center

Use a multi-touch mobile device application to explore the sounds made by instruments not available for hands-on exploration

Listen to a steady beat and repeat on a drum or xylophone

Identify piano and forte sounds

WRITING

Trace letters, numbers, and shapes on an interactive whiteboard

Create letters and numbers using playdough

Write and draw with sidewalk chalk

Introduce various purposes for writing

SOCIAL STUDIES

Partner with an upper-grade classroom to copublish an e-book on feelings

Take a neighborhood walk

Have family members visit the classroom to discuss family traditions

Work in small groups

Grade Level: First Grade

ART

Use a video camera to record children describing artwork and upload videos to the classroom website

Watch videos of artists explaining the thoughts behind their art

Observe differences and similarities between drawing and painting

Paint with intentional use of warm and cool colors

READING

Participate in guided reading groups

Record one's own reading and listen back to evaluate and reflect on fluency

Create opportunities to see self as an author

Use books to gather information for research

PHYSICAL EDUCATION

Participate in whole- and small-group organized games

Walk on a balance beam

Discuss the importance of rules in organized games

Use an iPad for small groups of students to view demonstrations of healthy stretches

HEALTH

Take photographs of children's food at home, and then sort into food groups

In small groups, discuss thoughtful food choices (for a day's eating)

Invite a guest speaker, such as a doctor or dentist, to visit the classroom to discuss healthy habits

Partner with family members in packing their own school lunch

LANGUAGE

Enable web-based literature experiences with One More Story or Tumblebooks to listen to fluent readers

Use discipline-specific vocabulary (for example, math and science terminology)

Develop the ability to read with inflection

Develop strategies to use language playfully (for example, creating jokes or riddles)

MUSIC

Sing a song while the teacher accompanies with an instrument

Read/sing children's e-books to a tune

Take a field trip to an orchestra

Handle and try out large instruments

MATH

Work tangram puzzles

Use a calculator (stand-alone or multi-touch mobile device) to help with basic computation

Explain the children's mental math processes

Use various tools for measuring

WRITING

Create video books

Write reminder notes for the class

Make books about things they know how to do

Write short notes or letters to others

SCIENCE

Create a worm and soil science center

Review nonfiction (children's magazines and books) about prehistoric life

Collect information in inquiry groups on planets in the solar system

Create radio show conversations about research on sea life

SOCIAL STUDIES

Explore cultures and families in regions of the world through viewing photographs and videos

Develop understandings of various currencies through handling and comparing money denominations

Tell stories of popular tales in other cultures

Observe different weather patterns over various regions of the world

Grade Level: Second Grade

ART

- Paint with intentional use of warm and cool colors
- Create a collage with a particular theme
- Allow students to use a multi-touch mobile device to photograph their pieces to create an art e-portfolio
- Make paintings of familiar locations throughout the neighborhood or community

PHYSICAL EDUCATION

- Watch videos of dancers: use as models to try new dance moves in small groups
- Participate in small-group organized games
- Compare familiar organized games with professional sports
- Invite a personal trainer as a guest speaker to discuss healthy exercise choices

LANGUAGE

- Record children doing book-review videos and share on a website
- Tell stories with logical beginning, middle, and ending events
- Engage with groups of children to discuss how they connected to events or literature
- Provide opportunities to begin interviewing others

MATH

- Read online weather charts to make predictions for future weather
- Observe symmetry by cutting fruit and vegetables in particular ways
- Practice math skills through games (boxed and web-based)
- Interact with money and coins

SCIENCE

- Create an e-newsletter in small groups that describes current investigations
- Take a field trip to a forest; gather field notes with an audio recording device
- Make sketches of plant life found in forests
- Explore how various systems operate (plumbing, railroad, schedules)

READING

- Read independently on Nook, Kindle, or other e-reader
- Complete word work at child's level
- Provide opportunities for children to describe themselves as readers
- Have small-group discussions exploring differences between genres

HEALTH

- Plan healthy meals to eat for a week
- Identify muscle groups
- Explore body systems and their functions
- Digitally record an exercise diary reflecting on attitudes and progress

MUSIC

- Record song sung by the class and accompanied by instruments played by students; release it to the public
- Explore individual interests with instruments
- Listen to singers and identify various voices (e.g., alto and soprano)
- Discuss how certain songs elicit certain feelings or emotions

WRITING

- Observe various nonfiction texts, features of newspapers, and magazine articles under a document camera
- Write accurate notes while conducting an interview
- Provide opportunities to see self and others as authors
- Use an assignment notebook to keep self organized

SOCIAL STUDIES

- Create a podcast of interviews with community members or school faculty
- Visit local community programs such as YMCA, Red Cross, and Boys and Girls Clubs
- Read informational articles about the harmful effects of littering
- Compare and contrast communities and cultures

Grade Level: Third Grade

ART

Use an iPad note-taking application to record notes during a field trip to an art museum

Provide opportunities to choose mediums for projects

Sketch areas of the neighborhood

Discuss connections and feelings associated with pieces of artwork in small groups

PHYSICAL EDUCATION

Create demonstration videos to exhibit techniques or strategies for a given game or sport

Play two team games in a given sport (e.g., baseball, basketball, hockey)

Develop organized games in small groups and teach to other groups

Provide opportunities to run longer distances

LANGUAGE

Discuss similarities and differences of stories

Create, perform, and digitally record a play or skit depicting individuals and roles from the past

Infuse new vocabulary into conversation with others

Participate in foreign language clubs

MATH

Demonstrate fractions with manipulatives under a document camera

Learn about communities by reading graphs and charts

Work through real-life problems using four operations

Develop games for others to demonstrate understanding of math skills

SCIENCE

Videoconference with an engineer to learn about the operation of machines

Monitor the use of energy in a classroom or building

Take a field trip to observe the system of printing a newspaper

Conduct research to explore food chains

READING

Read books on a Nook, Kindle, or other e-reader and discuss in book clubs

Read printed books and discuss in book clubs

Create individualized spelling lists with students and teachers

Recommend books to others

HEALTH

Keep a nutrition diary

Create a video health service announcement that shares statistics about obesity in the United States

Explore healthy activities and lifestyles

Research short- and long-term effects of smoking

MUSIC

Record interviews with singers, songwriters, and/or musicians

Perform solo and/or in groups using instruments

Utilize instruments or singing to exhibit knowledge and understanding in other disciplines

Explore how music can trigger a feeling or state of mind

WRITING

Send e-mails to experts on a given topic to aid in research

Write a story, including character dialogue

Write diary entries written from the perspective of people from the past or future

Infuse new vocabulary in writing

SOCIAL STUDIES

Explore divisions of the United States' government

Use digital cameras to take photographs of rural and urban neighborhoods during neighborhood walks to compare and contrast settings

Identify values and beliefs of various government systems

Explore how holidays support various cultural or governmental beliefs

My friend and colleague Bonnie Blagojevic, a research associate at the University of Maine Center for Community Inclusion and Disabilities Studies and active member of the NAEYC Technology and Young Children Interest Forum (http://techandyoungchildren.org), joins me in highlighting the importance of becoming aware of what developmentally appropriate technology integration looks like, feels like, and sounds like.

Technology is rapidly changing and influencing our daily lives and the lives of young children, both at home and in early education programs. What is our role as early childhood educators? Do we need to learn about technology in order to teach young children in this digital age?

I think we do. Why? Children are increasingly exposed to smartphones, mobile devices, digital cameras, computers, the Internet, and many other forms of technology in their daily lives. If we are to understand how technology can and does impact children, both in positive and negative ways, we need to know more about it ourselves. How else can we engage in meaningful and informed conversations with colleagues and family members searching for guidance regarding the appropriate use of technology with young children?

Will the selected technology be used to provide new access to learning and expression that is motivating, can support diverse learners, reflection, investigation, relationship building, and creation of art and music, and can help children "show what they know"? Or will it be used in ways that do not support what we believe are the kinds of early learning experiences that are best for the healthy growth and development of young children in our care?

To make decisions on when and how these new and emerging technology options can be beneficial for young children, we need to know more about technology and what research says about the use of these tools. We need to be familiar with technology ourselves and with technology standards and criteria to help with the selection of software, apps, and appropriate activities for using a particular technology. We need to have conversations about what we feel is important for a group of young children to learn, and to observe and assess how to help every child succeed.

When we are clear about our learning goals for children or a particular child *and* we understand what technology options are available and how they can be used to support identified goals, we are better equipped to make those important daily decisions. Which choices of traditional and/or technological learning materials will work best? Remember, as children learn concepts, one learning material may be best for one child and another for a different child, and/or the same child may benefit from one choice on one day and a different choice on another day.

Adults, as well as children, can use technology to "work smarter" and get things done, research information, communicate with colleagues, create, assess, and more. As people are increasingly connected through social networks, online communities, and technology, we all need to learn how to manage our media "diet" and to use technology in ways that are truly beneficial.

If we feel strongly about educational topics such as nature appreciation, play, language, diversity, and social-emotional development, let's consider how technology can support these priorities. Show children how to use nature webcams on the Internet to peek into an eagle's nest and watch eagles raise their young, observing and discussing what eagles eat, where they live, and how that connects with their own lives. Or teach children to use digital cameras to photograph their block constructions, print, and post them together with their stories and reflect with others about their creations. Collaborate by video chat with children and classrooms in other parts of the country or world, and/or use "video visiting" to involve distant family members with classroom projects. Use technology to enrich, not replace, hands-on learning experiences so important to young children.

To learn how to use technology intentionally in ways that will benefit young children, we need to continue to participate in ongoing conversations in our early childhood education communities as to how to take advantage of technology tools and use them well.

Bonnie acknowledges, like Chip and Andy, that technology is all around us. The wires of technology have joined the threads that make the fabric of our lives. She mentions maintaining conversations about technology use in the field of early childhood education. This can be done by teaming up with fellow teachers when trying new strategies. If you have colleagues in your school to talk with, start with them. You can also participate in discussions in the NAEYC Technology Interest Forum or the online Diigo group ECETECH, or attend workshops or conference sessions with technology-related content.

There are a few important points to consider when identifying activities to try in a classroom. To begin, survey what technology equipment is available. The Classroom Equipment Survey (form 1.3) can help you determine any piece of equipment that may be necessary to carry out an experience.

Next, you should identify what technological competencies you already possess. This will indicate any research and preparation you need to carry out an experience with a class. Use the Assessing Your Skills Sheet (form 1.4) to determine your existing competencies and what skills you need to learn. In

1.3 Classroom Equipment Survey

EQUIPMENT	PRESENT OR NOT PRESENT	LOCATION IN ROOM
Desktop Computer(s)	Present	Back Corner
Power Cable	Not Present	Back Corner
Laptop Computer(s)	Not Present	
Power Cable	Not Present	
Charge Cable	Not Present	
LCD Projector	Not Present	
Power Cable	Not Present	
VGA/HDMI Cable	Not Present	
Document Camera	Not Present	
Power Cable	Not Present	
VGA/HDMI Cable	Not Present	
Multi-Touch Mobile Device(s)	Present	Closet
Power Cable	Present	Closet
Charge Cable	Not Present	
VGA/HDMI Cable	Present	Desk Drawer
PC/Mac Connection Cable	Present	Desk Drawer
Printer(s)	Present	Back Corner
Power Cable	Present	Back Corner
Charge Cable	Present	Back Corner
PC/Mac Connection Cable	Present	Back Corner
Camcorder/Video Camera	Not Present	
Power Cable	Not Present	
Charge Cable	Not Present	
PC/Mac Connection Cable	Not Present	
Audio Recording Device(s)	Not Present	
Power Cable	Not Present	
PC/Mac Connection Cable	Not Present	
Speakers	Present	Classroom next door
Power Cable	Present	Classroom next door
PC/Mac Connection Cable	Present	Classroom next door
Batteries	Not Present	
Extension Cord(s)	Present	Custodian closet
Power Strip Cord(s)	Present	Near my desk

1.4 Assessing Your Skills Sheet

What do you know how to do?	What do you want to know how to do?	How will you learn how to do it?
Use my computer at home. Upload photographs to my computer at home. Upload music to my iPod. Log into iTunes. Email a friend. Print from my computer.	Have students in small groups write a classroom newsletter. Use a donated iPod in my listening center.	Work with a parent to manage children learning how to use the word processing programs. Talk to my administration about getting permission to put iTunes on my computer. Talk to my son about how to download iTunes to my school computer.

doing so, you will become aware of what knowledge you have and how to seek out the new knowledge needed to provide certain classroom experiences.

You also need to remain cognizant of the technological competencies that children possess. If children encounter activities that they are not ready for, they can become easily frustrated and likely to walk away from the activity (Stephen and Plowman 2008). This may result in less willingness to engage with technology in the future because they fear they may experience the same frustration.

After you have identified a few strategies you feel confident in implementing, determine where in your curriculum they will best fit. However, before doing so, you should have a firm grasp on the skills and concepts taught throughout the school year. The Curriculum Map (form 1.5) can be used to dissect a particular discipline and identify the skills and concepts children are to learn over a period of time. Organizing the curriculum in such a fashion provides you with a way to ensure that skills and concepts are addressed, paced appropriately, built on each other, and supportive of skills and concepts in grades to come. In my experience, and in the experience of my colleagues, developing curriculum maps in a collaborative framework

1.5 Curriculum Map

GRADE LEVEL: Kindergarten   DISCIPLINE/CONTENT AREA: Social Studies/Families

MONTH	SKILLS	ACTIVITIES
September	Everyone has a name. People are similar and different in many ways.	View cards with children's names written on them. View photographs of children in class.
October	Families are made up of people. Each family is different.	View photographs of children's families. Paint family portraits.
November	Families live in different places. Families celebrate different holidays and events.	View videos of the children celebrating different holidays and events in different cultures. Family members visit classroom to discuss their home.
December	Families sometimes have to travel to see other family members. People have traditions around certain times of the year.	Video conference with a classmate that is visiting family out of town. Share about times they visited family members out of town.
January	People enjoy doing different activities together during certain seasons. People celebrate the new year in different ways at various times of the year.	Project photographs and videos of people in China celebrating the new year. Guest speaker from another culture to share how they celebrate the new year.

provides a sense of support and a source of reflection. Also, when teachers work together to identify skills and concepts and sequence learning experiences, their practices can become more cohesive and connected. If your class is the only one of its age level, you may want to pair with a colleague at another school to develop curriculum maps. Though practices and experiences may not completely align due to variances in program focus, the collaboration and sense of support will help teachers develop confidence in the plan and their practice. Once you have developed a curriculum map or a similar plan, you can then thoughtfully insert elements of technology.

Introducing a Technology to the Children

It is important to show children how materials are to be used or how they are not to be used. When young children do not know how to use particular items, they may end up throwing or breaking them. A technology cart or station can be an expensive addition to your classroom, so it is vital to thoughtfully introduce it to the children so they will transfer the respect they have for other classroom items to the new items. It is also important to discuss how the technology will be used in the whole class and in small groups. Like all other classroom materials, when children know the purpose and value of the technology, they will know how to use it properly and are more likely to treat it with respect. Later, if situations do arise when equipment is not being handled appropriately, you have conversations to refer back to. For example, chapter 8 has additional information on how to introduce iPads and applications. This is necessary, because children will more than likely be using these devices independently.

Forms

①

1.1 Goal-Setting Sheet

www.redleafpress.org/tech/1-1.pdf

1.2 Planning for Student Equipment Use Sheet

www.redleafpress.org/tech/1-2.pdf

1.3 Classroom Equipment Survey

www.redleafpress.org/tech/1-3.pdf

1.4 Assessing Your Skills Sheet

www.redleafpress.org/tech/1-4.pdf

1.5 Curriculum Map

www.redleafpress.org/tech/1-5.pdf

1.1 Goal-Setting Sheet

Measurable and Manageable Goal:

Date:

PLAN TO COMPLETE GOAL

Equipment I need to obtain:

Skills I need to learn:

Individuals I need to collaborate/communicate with:

Evidence goal has been achieved:

REFLECTION IF GOAL WAS NOT MET

Obstacles encountered:

Plan to overcome the obstacles:

Future goal(s):

1.2 Planning for Student Equipment Use Sheet

Equipment being used:

Learning experiences using equipment over the course of the year:

Learning experiences using equipment during the following dates:

How the children will be using the equipment (independently/small groups):

Skills that need to be taught in the next week:

Skills that need to be taught in the upcoming months:

Plan for the upcoming months:

Evidence of plan completion:

1.3 Classroom Equipment Survey

EQUIPMENT	PRESENT OR NOT PRESENT	LOCATION IN ROOM
Desktop Computer(s)		
Power Cable		
Laptop Computer(s)		
Power Cable		
Charge Cable		
LCD Projector		
Power Cable		
VGA/HDMI Cable		
Document Camera		
Power Cable		
VGA/HDMI Cable		
Multi-Touch Mobile Device(s)		
Power Cable		
Charge Cable		
VGA/HDMI Cable		
PC/Mac Connection Cable		
Printer(s)		
Power Cable		
Charge Cable		
PC/Mac Connection Cable		
Camcorder/Video Camera		
Power Cable		
Charge Cable		
PC/Mac Connection Cable		
Audio Recording Device(s)		
Power Cable		
PC/Mac Connection Cable		
Speakers		
Power Cable		
PC/Mac Connection Cable		
Batteries		
Extension Cord(s)		
Power Strip Cord(s)		

1.4 Assessing Your Skills Sheet

What do you know how to do?	What do you want to know how to do?	How will you learn how to do it?

1.5 Curriculum Map

GRADE LEVEL: _____ DISCIPLINE/CONTENT AREA: _____

MONTH	SKILLS	ACTIVITIES
September		
October		
November		
December		
January		

1.5 Curriculum Map

GRADE LEVEL: _____ DISCIPLINE/CONTENT AREA: _____

MONTH	SKILLS	ACTIVITIES
February		
March		
April		
May		
June		

2
Using Photographs and Images to Inspire

www.redleafpress.org/tech/2-1.aspx

On February 2, 2011, a blizzard laid twenty inches of snow across the city of Chicago. The immense snowfall slowed traffic to a stop, and cars became buried as they sat in traffic. On Lakeshore Drive, some five hundred cars had to be abandoned, leaving an eerie stretch of empty cars for miles. Chicago Public Schools closed for two days, the first time in over twelve years. As people emerged from their homes to investigate, they took out their cameras and camcorders to capture the chilling sights. Photos and videos appeared all over the Internet and television. These graphic photos and videos provided people around the country with an opportunity to share in the scary, yet amazing, experience.

The day after the storm hit, I took a walk to survey the snow myself. I brought my camera with me to capture what I saw. As I trudged through the snow, I held my camera, looking for scenes to capture. I snapped photos I could e-mail to family throughout the country, warning my family in Vermont and Maine of what was to come. I photographed cars buried up to their windows, snowmobiles tossing snow in the air, and meandering trails people had shoveled in front of their houses. I photographed snow completely covering

garage doors, trapping cars inside. I photographed strange items along the roadside, such as logs, chairs, benches, milk crates, sticks, coolers, planters, picnic baskets, and even two houseplants.

I thought this picture was particularly interesting, because only residents of densely populated urban areas would understand the significance of such items. I decided to take this photo to my classroom to show the preschoolers. I wondered what questions the children would generate from observing such a strange scene and what discussion might ensue. I wondered if, in their life experience thus far, they understood the significance of chairs and houseplants in snow.

When schools were reopened and the three- and four-year-olds and I returned to our classroom, I projected several photographs on a large screen for the children to see. I invited them to look closely at the photos and share their observations. As we discussed their observations, their understanding of city culture became quite evident.

Me: Boys and girls, I want to make sure that you see the chair and the houseplants in this photograph. Why do you think they are there?

Hannah: Those things are there because the people are saving the spots.

Me: Can you tell us more about that and what you mean?

Hannah: Well, those people shoveled very hard and worked very hard and don't want anyone to take their spots, so they are saving it with that stuff. My dad shoveled last night and saved a spot with buckets and a broom. It was his first time, though, and he was kind of nervous about doing it. He didn't know if his spot was going to get taken or not.

Hannah clearly understood complex ideas surrounding saving spots and why people do it. Moreover, she was able to articulate this understanding by connecting family experiences to a photograph depicting popular winter culture in the city of Chicago.

Photographs capture moments in time. Not only do they capture color, events, and people, but they also capture culture, understanding, emotion, and ideas. People respond to photographs as an opportunity to revisit a moment in the past, such as a baby's first steps, a milestone birthday, or a family vacation. When this happens, people engage in familiar discussions about people, events, and stories associated with memories.

When children look at photographs, they use their background knowledge and experiences to process them. Since young children have limited background knowledge and experiences, it's not always possible to anticipate what they will say. What children do share, however, provides teachers with a wealth of knowledge in terms of how children process information, utilize vocabulary, and create connections. Presenting photographs in the context of learning offers children an opportunity to deeply explore familiar ideas and start investigating novel ones. Photographs can build a bridge for students to connect the familiar to the unfamiliar. They inspire a sense of awe and wonder. The clarity and authentic details offered in photographs allow students to imagine what it would feel like to be in the place depicted in the photo. It's possible to imagine what it would feel like under a hot sun in the Sahara Desert or sailing on the crisp waters of the Atlantic Ocean. When children are exposed to sketches or clip art, they are not able to observe the details and textures that are present in photographs. Observing photographs helps children develop accurate mental images that they can call on in the future to provide background knowledge and support for new learning. Here's an example.

Take a look at the photograph of the Chicago skyline. Consider these questions as discussion points.

- What colors do you see?

- What do you think the weather is like on this day? How do you know?

- What season do you think this photograph was taken in?

- Do you think it was a windy day when this photograph was taken?

- Where do you think the photographer was standing when this photograph was taken?

- After looking at this image, would you want to visit this city?

- What do you think the bird is doing in the photograph?

Now try this exercise again, using the same set of questions, while looking at this sketch.

Where sketches have value in particular learning experiences, photographs can help children make high-level connections and develop a sense of inquiry in science, for example. The sketch does not help children make observations about the weather or the various building structures in the skyline. The sketch also does not provide detail for exploring various shoreline structures or animal life in this region of the United States.

Using Photographs to Support Learning

People are accustomed to using cameras to capture memories during a family reunion, holiday celebration, birthday, or graduation. Cameras can be used to capture important moments in a classroom as well. These moments can be used to support children's learning in a variety of ways. As I described earlier, a single device can serve several purposes. Photographs can be used in classrooms to

- ✓ facilitate conversation,
- ✓ develop emotional vocabulary,
- ✓ model desired behaviors,
- ✓ recall a learning experience,
- ✓ develop schema,
- ✓ help children inspire other children,
- ✓ explore the neighborhood,
- ✓ build classroom and school community,
- ✓ learn about authors, and
- ✓ share other communities and cultures.

FACILITATE CONVERSATION

Photographs can be used in creative ways to have conversations in order to meet a variety of goals and objectives. When young children have the opportunity to take time to observe, their brains process the content within the photographs. Their eyes scan and rescan the photograph, looking for things that seem familiar and studying those things that are not. After children have been given time to observe, they need time to discuss. For young children, transforming thoughts into spoken words is a developing cognitive task that requires time. Therefore, teachers should give children time to make this transformation and share with those around them. Given the varying backgrounds and developmental levels of young children, they will need various levels of assistance in expressing their ideas.

When facilitating conversations around photographs, it may be helpful to share a few connections you have to the photograph. After modeling the thinking and speaking process, invite the children to share their ideas. You can begin the conversation by posing questions or sharing potential connections. Photographs provide an authentic context that allows teachers to introduce new words. Use photographs to inspire conversations that allow children time to learn and utilize vocabulary to express their ideas.

DEVELOP EMOTIONAL VOCABULARY

Young children need to learn vocabulary to articulate feelings and emotions in order to develop self-regulation. You can facilitate emotional vocabulary development by providing children with the opportunity to identify facial expressions in photographs and have a conversation about the emotion each person is depicting.

Young children are developing the ability to utilize strategies to regulate their emotions. Take photographs of each child showing a specific feeling, and share them with the class. Sharing these photographs will help the children learn that though particular feelings are felt by everyone, their facial expressions are all a bit different. Additionally, as the children interact with one another, they will begin to see these facial expressions on their classmates and already have an idea of what other children are feeling at a particular moment. This lays the foundation for teaching resolution skills as students learn to interpret and react to facial expressions.

MODEL DESIRED BEHAVIORS

Young children need thoughtful modeling when you are introducing new concepts, skills, or routines. Photographs can model desired behaviors in a classroom. When introducing a technology center to a classroom, you can frame

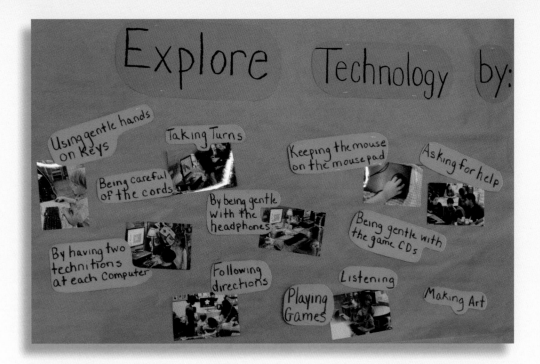

the introduction by "We will explore technology by . . ." rather than discussing how children should not explore technology. When guidelines are framed in what children should do, an element of accountability is built in. The guidelines provide a framework to return to when children are found doing other things with materials.

Consider the following as an example to encourage particular practices in a technology center.

We Explore Technology by . . .

Using gentle hands on the mouse, keyboard, and headphones.

Sharing and taking turns.

Asking for help when we need it.

Working independently or with classmates.

After guidelines have been established, you can begin observing the children at the technology center with a camera in hand. While observing, take photographs of children carrying out the desired tasks. Print these photographs, and post them on a bulletin board next to the guidelines. After doing so, gather the children around the center and discuss what was observed. Acknowledge that snapshots were taken when children were seen behaving as they should at the center. Conclude the discussion with an invitation to use the board when they have forgotten what they are to do at the technology center. It may also be helpful to invite the children to use the board as a resource when they notice other children not following the given guidelines.

RECALL A LEARNING EXPERIENCE

Photos can be used to remind children of concepts taught or learned the previous day or even earlier in the school year. Take photos of children working during a particular lesson and then later; refer back to the photographs to discuss how the children were or were not successful in completing a particular task. In a kindergarten classroom, a teacher took photographs of students while they were exploring objects through a poet's eyes by listing descriptive words for each particular object. The following day, the teacher showed a brief slide show of the students engaged in the previous day's work. As the students observed the photos, the teacher acknowledged examples of learning and on-task behaviors. "Notice how Carly is carefully examining that leaf," and "I can see Leo thinking before he writes his observations." Using these photos to activate students' memory set the tone for the upcoming lesson. The teacher used this activity to close the gap between yesterday and today and quickly reestablished students' productivity and focus from the previous day. Please be sure to privately ask for permission from any child you wish to single out in a situation like this. We cannot assume that all children like public attention, even when it is positive.

DEVELOP SCHEMA

At any level through third grade, teachers can use photographs to help children develop schema for content-area investigations. When children are given time to observe, think, and reflect, they are given the time they need to build background knowledge necessary for a unit of study. For a unit on outer space,

Young children are developing larger capacities for short- and long-term memory. Teachers can support this development while acknowledging and connecting day-to-day events.

a teacher can provide large photographs of planets and phenomena of the universe.

If photographs are not available, thoughtfully chosen books with authentic photographs can lend themselves to a similar experience. Children can visit these photographs and record their observations and questions on sticky notes or think sheets such as the Background Knowledge Think Sheet (form 2.1). The structure of these experiences is intentionally crafted to support varying paces of observing, thinking, writing, and drawing.

First-grade teacher Meghan Residori searched for authentic resources to help her class build background knowledge for an inquiry unit on worms. She provided books about soil and opportunities to hold and observe real worms in a classroom science center. Her class had a variety of worms that they wanted to learn about, but Meghan was surprised to find a lack of age-appropriate nonfiction literature on specific worm species. In order to provide the authentic resources that she wanted, she went out in search of photographs of the worms her class wanted to learn about. As the children observed the photographs she found, they wrote down specific questions and observations. Later in their investigation, the class used the photographs to create observational drawings while

2.1 Background Knowledge Think Sheet

Name: Jaelyn

Write or draw any interesting ideas or observations:

All the planets seem round to me. That is interesting.
All the planets are different colors.
Some of the planets have what look like rings around them.

Write or draw any questions that you have:

What are the rings around the planets made out of?
How far apart are the planets from each other?
What is the most dangerous planet for a human to be on?
What is the safest planet for a human to be on?
I wonder if humans will ever reach the furthest planets . . .

developing an understanding of specific structures and colors. Once they had developed this understanding, they created diagrams and labeled the specific parts of the worms they learned about. In this experience, children used the photographs to explore new concepts and develop necessary shared background knowledge for an upcoming unit of investigation.

HELP CHILDREN INSPIRE OTHER CHILDREN

Kindergarten teacher Sarah Stegmaier believes that a block center can offer a whole host of valuable opportunities for language, social interactions, and the development of spatial sense. When she noticed her class was taking great interest in creating houses, she wanted to find a way to preserve the hard work and effort the children were putting into their construction. So Sarah began taking photographs of the houses. She posted these photographs in the block center as inspiration for future projects or to provide an opportunity to rebuild the same houses at a later date. Once the children became familiar with Sarah taking photographs of their houses, Sarah put the camera in the hands of the children. Soon, they were taking their own photographs, paying close attention to the angle and quality of the photographs. Sarah keeps these photographs in the block center from year to year. At the beginning of the year, she uses these photographs to introduce the block center, providing examples of how children in the past have used the blocks. At this year-long classroom practice, children develop an understanding of what photographs can be used for. They also learn that their efforts can be preserved in a photograph that they and others can enjoy throughout the school year.

EXPLORE THE NEIGHBORHOOD

Within the scope and sequence of social studies in early childhood education, children will explore their neighborhood and community. Colleague Erin Stanfill, a preschool teacher, used photography to help her preschoolers learn about their neighborhood. To stimulate talk about their neighborhood, she shared several photographs of the neighborhood that she had taken. Erin took her class on a walking field trip around the neighborhood and gave the children an opportunity to take photographs of interesting things they observed. After their walk, she printed the photographs and invited the photographers to share them with the class. Erin noticed how this activity motivated her class to want to explore and discover more about their neighborhood. She also noticed that her camera needed to be replaced.

She collaborated with her grade-level partner to develop ideas for how to raise funds for new cameras. Erin informed her class that in order to continue photographing the neighborhood, they needed to raise money for new cameras. As a class, they decided to host a silent auction and sell the photographs they had already taken. Erin and her grade-level partner went to local businesses and advertised their event. Many neighborhood and community members attended the silent auction with the children and their families. Each child wore a "Photographer" badge and was available to answer questions from potential buyers. After the event concluded, enough money had been raised to purchase new cameras for their classrooms. Since the children had worked hard to raise money, they were extra careful when working with the new cameras.

Photography contributed to the high interest the children had in learning about their neighborhood. Note, too, that Erin included the children in the entire process of raising funds to obtain the necessary resources to continue photographing and learning about their neighborhood. This experience not only helped the children learn about their neighborhood, but it also helped the children develop a value and respect for cameras and photographs.

BUILD CLASSROOM AND SCHOOL COMMUNITY

Displaying photographs of the families present in a classroom sends an important message that the children in this room are important and their families are equally important. To do this, you can create a "Family Scrapbook" and display the photographs on a wall or bulletin board near an area where families frequently visit. At the beginning of the year, invite all the families to send in a photograph of their family.

Carli McKenney's preschool class is introduced to viewing photographs on an iPad. (*www.redleafpress.org /tech/2-2.aspx*)

For those children who do not send in a photograph, try to take a quick snapshot of the child and a parent at a family event, drop-off, or pickup. Before putting the photographs up, build excitement around the photographs by holding an event where the children can both exhibit their own and browse the other photographs. This provides each child with the opportunity to introduce the important people in their lives and helps the children get to know one another. When sharing, the children begin to learn similarities and differences about one another. They will begin to establish connections, which are meaningful catalysts for friendship.

When young children begin school, the new faces

can be overwhelming. You can help acquaint children with the other adults and children in the building by providing photographs of the other teachers and staff, paired with a note about what they do in the school. The smaller photo on the previous page is taken from a book made for a preschool classroom that identifies the role of each staff member, ranging from the principals to lunchroom staff. This book is introduced on the first day of school and read several times throughout the first weeks of school. Over time, the children begin to understand the role of the other adults in the building and also gain an understanding of the school community and culture.

It is not uncommon for families to expand as the year progresses. When this happens, you can welcome photographs of the new family member. The sibling in the classroom can share the new photographs with the class. After sharing the photographs, create a special interest center housing all of the photographs of the new family member. The sibling in the classroom can be the "expert" and answer any questions his or her peers may have about the new family member.

LEARN ABOUT AUTHORS

High-quality early childhood classrooms are rich in children's literature. It is important that teachers help young children connect to authors in a multitude of ways. You can find photographs of authors on their websites and then use them as a springboard for conversations with the children about an author's interests, family, pets, and more. As the children learn relevant and meaningful content about authors through photographs, the children begin to learn that authors are indeed relatable people.

When young children realize that authors are relatable, the idea of trying on the role of an author or illustrator becomes attainable. When these photographs are not being used as discussion pieces, they can be displayed in inexpensive frames in a classroom reading corner or library or taped to a book tub displaying books by the author. These practices reinforce the connections between text and the people who write them. Author studies are an amazing way to connect young children with authors.

Many children's authors are published in several languages. Todd Parr, for example, has books published in Spanish, Japanese, French, Chinese, Finnish, Greek, Portuguese, and Arabic. Laura Numeroff has several of her books published in Afrikaans, German, Hebrew, and Italian. When children observe photographs of these book covers, they will see differences in the letters, words, and sometimes cover designs. Through conversation with teachers and peers, they will learn that different languages are found across the globe. Building on that, the children will learn that familiar books are enjoyed by children all over the world.

Through read-alouds and other experiences with an author's texts, you can help children observe elements of an author's style. You can also do this with illustrators. Mo Willems is an author and illustrator. Willems is famous for his Knuffle Bunny books, inspired by his daughter, Trixie. Through reading these books, children will see that Willems uses photographs to create his illustrations. You can facilitate discussions with children about why Willems chose certain photos for particular pages. These discussions will help children learn that illustrations are related to the text on a page.

You can build on this learning by encouraging children to try on the roles of writing and illustrating a book inspired by Mo Willems's style. As a class, generate ideas for a story line. Give each child the opportunity to add an event to the story. After each child has created an event for the story, discuss what photograph would be needed to illustrate that event. You can help children identify photographs that illustrate their events by looking back at Willems's illustrations to see the connections between his photographs and the text. After the children have identified a photograph that best illustrates the event, invite the children to take the photographs needed for their page. You can do this by helping children take photographs of spaces in the school or neighborhood. Enlist the help of families by sending cameras home with children to capture a particular snapshot. Once the photographs have been taken and printed, children can use art supplies to create characters to be laid over the top of their photograph. Be sure to discuss how small or large the characters should be in order to fit on the photograph. Decide how you will publish this book: laminating, scanning and printing, or a photo book. Strategies for using Shutterfly and Snapfish for photo books are described in chapter 6.

Four-year-old Eddie talks with Brian Puerling about his experiences taking and viewing photographs on a multi-touch mobile device. (*www.redleafpress.org/tech/2-3.aspx*)

This experience does a number of valuable things for children. It helps them understand the hard work and time it takes to write, illustrate, and publish a book. It also provides an authentic and meaningful vehicle in which they can try on the roles of an author and illustrator.

In preschool and kindergarten classrooms, dramatic play provides an opportunity for young children to develop a multitude of skills and concepts in a fashion that is interesting and developmentally appropriate. Too often dramatic play centers are left to be a "housekeeping corner" limiting the roles, perspectives, concepts, and skills children can explore. In first-grade through third-grade classrooms, teachers can have children create skits, radio shows, or interviews from the perspective of prominent figures or roles. Teachers need to consider the importance of knowing other roles in the community, city, state, country, nation, and world.

SHARE OTHER COMMUNITIES AND CULTURES

A content-area unit on Australia can seem abstract to children in Chicago, but a dramatic play center can provide the children with an opportunity to access and explore life in Australia. An Australian Outback can be an engaging dramatic play center if children are involved in the entire construction process. Teachers can show children photographs of actual Outback landscapes. Children can observe photographs of animals commonly found in the Australian Outback. While looking at the photographs, children can point out observations and pose questions about what they are seeing.

As the children observe, they can discuss what it would feel like to take a ride in a jeep in the sweltering heat of the Outback. The children can discuss what Australian animals they would want to photograph if they were to take such a ride. After the children have viewed the photographs, discuss how what they have seen and learned about the Australian Outback can help them develop a list of items needed to construct an Australian Outback dramatic play center. Invite the children to draw things they observed in the photographs. Children who can write should label their work. After the children have completed their drawings, record what they think should be included in the Outback. Once the list is written, devise a plan with your class for how the dramatic play area will be transformed. Establish jobs that children can do to contribute to the construction of the Outback. By the time the Outback is open, the children will have established the necessary back knowledge with which to explore the skills and concepts in the dramatic play center. This background knowledge, paired with the dramatic play experience, provides opportunities for high-level play, which will help children learn and appreciate Australian animals. In this or a similar experience, the photographs offer the children important information about how the Outback looks and feels. They also offer information about the animals present in the Outback and what that might mean if someone were to encounter them. The photographs also encourage conversation about the necessary safety precautions when exploring the Outback.

When choosing photographs that portray other communities' cultures, be sure that the photographs are thoughtful representations. Be sure that the photographs do not perpetuate biases or stereotypes of a particular culture or region. Consider pairing with another teacher when searching for such photographs to reduce the likelihood of your own biases interfering with the selection of photographs.

Using Photographs to Support Assessment

Photographs offer a glimpse into concepts, communities, and cultures; therefore photographs will always be authentic instructional materials for early childhood educators. When you use photographs as instructional materials, continually observe and listen to how the children interact with the photographs. When you observe and listen carefully, you can learn how a child's ideas evolve over time. The forms in this chapter can be used to record information as children interact with photographs to determine children's background knowledge for particular topics. Reflective frameworks are also helpful to use when reviewing photographs to determine the effectiveness of activities, routines, and daily transitions. Teachers can use photographs to assess

✓ schema,

✓ effectiveness of activities, routines, and transitions, and

✓ knowledge of geometric shapes.

When young children work in small groups, they are generally given the opportunity to engage with concepts more concretely because they can handle materials, ask questions, announce observations, and hear other children's questions and comments. This deep engagement is necessary for children to understand information and concepts. This engagement develops interest and motivation, which naturally leads to inquiry processes. Although small groups are a developmentally appropriate dynamic for children to engage with concepts and materials, it is often difficult for a teacher to rotate through each group to provide the highest level of scaffolding and questioning.

SCHEMA

Teachers can assess children's background knowledge in a couple of ways: in the moment and after the moment. In the moment, a teacher can assess children's schema by recording their ideas using the At-a-Glance Background Knowledge Assessment (form 2.2). For example, if a small group of kindergarten children are observing a photograph of the Washington Monument, the teacher should listen closely to the questions the children ask, the observations they point out, and the connections they make. If the teacher hears a child ask, "Why is there a big stick coming out of the ground?" and then another child responds with, "That is not a stick. I have been there, and it was made for a president who lived a long time ago. It's a big deal," that teacher would learn important information about these two children. She would learn that the second child has visited the Washington Monument and is somewhat aware of

2.2 At-a-Glance Background Knowledge Assessment

Unit of Study: Important United States sculptures, statues, and locations

Common observations/questions recorded:

There are a lot of people looking at the tall building.

Why are there so many people there to see it?

How tall is the Washington Monument?

Unique or interesting observations/questions recorded:

Why is there a big stick coming out of the ground?

Misconceptions recorded:

A popular monument confused for a large stick

Notes for future teaching (areas for focus):

More experience looking at monuments

Find additional nonfiction books that describe the monuments.

Specific children to follow up with:

Ashley needs some additional experiences observing photographs.

She could benefit from using a magnifying glass when looking at actual photographs.

She could also benefit from zooming in on photographs while looking at them on a multi-touch mobile device.

the significance of it. She would learn that the child has some knowledge of vocabulary used to describe political figures and time. She would learn that the first child has little background knowledge or experience with important structures significant to the United States. She might also learn that the child may need some additional experiences with size relationships and constructed objects versus natural objects.

2.3 Individual Background Knowledge Assessment

Name: Ashley

Unit of Study: Important United States sculptures, statues, and locations

Observations/Questions:

A popular monument confused for a large stick

Why is there a big stick coming out of the ground?

Concept Awareness:

Sticks are often long and pointed.

Ashley is applying a concept to a context that does not make sense.

NOTES FOR FUTURE TEACHING:

Concepts to Learn:

How to better observe photographs

How to better use background knowledge to develop questions

Activities/Experiences to Teach Concepts:

She could benefit from using a magnifying glass when looking at actual photographs.

She could also benefit from zooming in on photographs while looking at them on a multi-touch mobile device.

After the moment, a teacher can use the Individual Background Knowledge Assessment (form 2.3) to explore a particular child's background knowledge. Teachers can record important information on the assessment while reviewing any sticky notes written by the child. Through review of children's notes, teachers can also identify misconceptions to be addressed before continuing an in-depth unit of study.

EFFECTIVENESS OF ACTIVITIES, ROUTINES, AND TRANSITIONS

In any classroom, the teacher, assistant, or volunteer can take photographs as children move throughout the room during various activities. Later, teachers can review the photographs while thinking about important questions using either the Photograph Reflection Checklist for preschool or kindergarten and early elementary (forms 2.4 and 2.5).

Answering the questions on the form can provide a wealth of knowledge. You will learn whether you need to restructure daily schedules, change out supplies, reteach the use of particular supplies, reorganize the classroom layout, or redesign goals and objectives for particular centers.

It is very helpful to review the photographs with grade-level partners, teams of teachers across grade levels, or a mentor teacher. The opportunity to learn from other professionals is something that should never be passed up. Together, the group can identify patterns across classrooms and age groups and brainstorm solutions to challenging areas. Reviewing photographs in such a structure can also help you identify routines, transitions, or teacher practices that could use more cohesion across grade levels.

2.4 Photograph Reflection Checklist: Preschool

Photograph's Contents: Photographs of children during the self-selected center portion of the day.

Date(s): 5/25/2011 Midmorning

Reflection Questions	Yes	No
Are the children able to easily move through the room?	X	
Which centers are not being utilized? writing center is not	X	
Does it appear that all the centers are providing enough materials for those visiting? Do any materials need to be updated or replaced?	X	
Are there any patterns in how children choose which centers to visit?		X
Does it appear that children are able to focus on the given tasks?	X	
Does it appear that children are able to work collaboratively with the given space and materials?	X	
Are there any areas of the room that appear to have obstructed views due to furniture or other fixtures?	X	
Are the given center tasks addressing early learning standards?	X	

To-Do List	Plan to Complete
Conduct additional observations with a focus on the writing center to explore why children are not visiting it. Conduct observations again on Thursday and Friday.	Speak with children informally over lunch and indicate that I have noticed that children have not been visiting the writing center and see what they say.

2.5 Photograph Reflection Checklist: Kindergarten and Early Elementary

Photograph's Contents: Children during their literacy centers

Date(s): 3/16/2011

Reflection Questions	Yes	No
Are the children able to easily move through the room?	X	
Which centers are not being utilized? all being utilized		X
Does it appear that all the centers are providing enough materials for those visiting? Do any materials need to be updated or replaced?	X	
Are there any patterns in how children choose which centers to visit?		X
Does it appear that children are able to focus on the given tasks?	X	
Does it appear that children are able to work collaboratively with the given space and materials? Word Wall Work Center looks too small		X
Are there any areas of the room that appear to have obstructed views due to furniture or other fixtures?		X
Are the given center tasks addressing early learning standards?	X	
Does the center time structure appear to facilitate independent and small-group work?	X	
Does it appear that children are able to independently access the materials needed for their centers (independent or small-group work)?	X	
Are children working in small groups remaining on task?	X	

To-Do List	Plan to Complete
Identify where other teachers have their Word Walls. Explore other Word Wall Work Center management systems.	Speak with the other kindergarten teachers to see where they have their Word Walls. Ask them how they manage its use during their literacy center time.

KNOWLEDGE OF GEOMETRIC SHAPES

Teachers can use child-friendly cameras to help assess a child's knowledge of geometric shapes. In small groups, children can embark on a scavenger hunt around a classroom, school, or neighborhood with a camera and a list of shapes to capture digitally. After the groups have taken their photographs, the photographs can be projected onto a screen to be shared with the rest of the class. While the groups share their photographs, the teacher can learn about the children's abilities to observe their environments and identify particular shapes.

Using Photographs to Exhibit Learning

Photographs offer a viewer a glimpse of a moment in time. Within this glimpse, teachers and families can learn a whole host of important things about a child. By observing a photograph, they could learn whether a child can kick a ball, jump rope, build a tower, work cooperatively with another child, write a number, or use scissors. Capture these moments and share them with important individuals to exhibit what children are learning. Teachers can exhibit learning using photographs through

- ✓ e-photo portfolios,
- ✓ school functions, and
- ✓ classroom websites.

E-PHOTO PORTFOLIOS

Creating student portfolios is not an unfamiliar practice, but more efficient ways of creating, maintaining, organizing, and sharing them exist using today's technologies. Teachers can create e-photo portfolios by collecting photographs of children and sorting them into student files on a computer, laptop, or multi-touch mobile device. During parent-teacher conferences, e-photo portfolios can be reviewed in conjunction with work samples. Reviewing these materials provides a clearer picture of a child's development across disciplines. Work samples show the *product* of progress over time, and photographs show the *process* of progress over time. In creating e-photo portfolios of children, teachers have an accessible and portable portfolio that can be shared with much more flexibility than traditional manila folder portfolios.

E-photo portfolios can also be used as a tool for individualized goal setting. While reviewing photographs, you can take notes on an E-Photo Portfolio Goal-Setting Planner (form 2.6) to help organize observations and goals for future teaching and learning. The planner can be filled out electronically on a computer or a multi-touch mobile device and then housed in the child's e-portfolio. The presence of the planner in the e-portfolio provides a lens with which to observe the included materials.

In every classroom, there are always a few children who become a concern. When you have specific concerns about a child, an e-photo portfolio offers a comprehensive view of the child's current level of development. An e-photo portfolio can provide evidence of a need for assistance when seeking help from specialists or other professionals.

2.6 E-Photo Portfolio Goal-Setting Planner

Child: Ella
Grade: Preschool
Marking Period: Winter
Date: January 13, 2011

Based on the photographs reviewed, skills exhibited include:

Ella is able to successfully engage in organized activities with older children.
She appears to know how to hold a book.
She appears to enjoy engaging with books.

Based on the photographs reviewed, skills that need to be addressed include:

Letting others take turns in organized games when working with children her age

Activities/Experiences:		Dates:
1	Play a game one-on-one with a friend.	Friday of this week
2	Play a game with two other children.	Thursday morning of next week
3		

SCHOOL FUNCTIONS

Many schools hold open houses and parent-teacher conferences. At these events, every family wants to talk with the teacher, so they often end up standing around waiting. While families wait to talk with you, they can watch a five-minute slideshow of photographs depicting classroom learning experiences. Slide shows can offer families a quick overview of the year, a field trip, or a unit of study. Software programs like iPhoto for Apple computers come with the ability to organize photos into a slide show quickly and easily. Teachers can also take photographs and create elaborate videos or movies that allow you to add written and verbal descriptions of experiences shown in the photographs.

Software programs found on standard computers, such as iMovie and Windows Movie Maker, are user-friendly for such projects.

CLASSROOM WEBSITES

While e-photo portfolios are for private viewing and may contain confidential information, photographs that are not confidential can be shared on classroom websites. Shutterfly and Snapfish are photo-album organizers. The Shutterfly website offers users the ability to create websites that share not only photographs but also videos, web links, book recommendations, and downloadable handouts. You can create a website in a format and fashion that suits the needs of the children and families in your classroom. Sorting photographs

into albums by centers, learning experiences, and events makes the website easily navigable for visitors. When creating albums and sorting photographs, you can create titles for albums so the contents are clear to visitors. Beyond the title, you can provide a description of the album, which can help families understand what they are viewing and allow you to maintain a digital scrapbook that can be viewed over time.

Families can view photographs and create keepsake items with just a few clicks. Whenever posting photographs of children online, you should make sure that a school or classroom media release form has been signed by families. Beyond that, public viewing is also an issue. Shutterfly provides a security option that places a password on the website, making it viewable only to those to whom the password has been given. I suggest changing the password each year to ensure security for each new group of families.

◆　　◆　　◆

Photographs may seem simple, but when used thoughtfully and intentionally, they offer children, teachers, and families valuable information about individuals, skills, concepts, neighborhoods, communities, and cultures. A photograph is an amazing item that can jump-start meaningful conversations among a group of children, a group of educators, or a parent and a teacher. Photographs in early childhood classrooms provide children with opportunities to build background knowledge. They provide teachers with the ability to reflect on and learn about the children in their classrooms. They also provide families with the answers to many questions they would traditionally ask educators.

You may fear that cameras and other technologies distract children from their engagement or learning. As a means to reduce the distractions, educators tend to try and sneak photographs of children. This, however, only increases the distractions. Children become distracted when they do not understand something in their environment. For example, if a teacher is reading a story and the principal walks in, many of the children's heads will turn and remain turned. In their minds, they are seeking to understand the presence of the principal by asking themselves, "Why is she here? What will she say? Who is in trouble?" Children seek to understand events and situations, so it's important to introduce technology to children and explain to them how it will be used. For cameras, teachers need to inform children that the classroom camera(s) will be used to create memories on exciting days, capture moments when they have learned something new, and share information with others. When this is done carefully and intentionally, children will understand the presence of the camera at any time. This will in turn reduce the distractions of engagement.

» **TOOLBOX TIPS**

CHOOSING A NEW CAMERA

New cameras are coming out each day. When looking for a camera, it is important to think about what you want in a camera. Ask yourself these questions to begin your search for the right camera:

- What do you know about digital cameras?
- Do you want a camera that simply points and shoots?
- Do you want a camera with significant zoom abilities?
- What types of photographs do you plan to take?
- Where will you be taking photographs?
- Who will be using the camera?
- Do you want a camera with options that allow you to adjust settings for picture quality?
- Do you want a camera that requires software installation?
- What type of computer will you use to organize the photographs?
- What is your price range?

After answering these questions, take your notes to an electronics store to discuss them with a camera specialist. The information provided to the specialist will be helpful in finding the right camera. If you are interested in purchasing a camera online, websites such as www.buy.com, www.overstock.com, and www.tigerdirect.com will be helpful in finding a camera at a significantly lower price.

Forms

2.1 Background Knowledge Think Sheet

www.redleafpress.org/tech/2-1.pdf

2.2 At-a-Glance Background Knowledge Assessment

www.redleafpress.org/tech/2-2.pdf

2.3 Individual Background Knowledge Assessment

www.redleafpress.org/tech/2-3.pdf

2.4 Photograph Reflection Checklist: Preschool

www.redleafpress.org/tech/2-4.pdf

2.5 Photograph Reflection Checklist: Kindergarten and Early Elementary

www.redleafpress.org/tech/2-5.pdf

2.6 E-Photo Portfolio Goal-Setting Planner

www.redleafpress.org/tech/2-6.pdf

2.1 Background Knowledge Think Sheet

Name:

Write or draw any interesting ideas or observations:

Write or draw any questions that you have:

2.2 At-a-Glance Background Knowledge Assessment

Unit of Study:

Common observations/questions recorded:

Unique or interesting observations/questions recorded:

Misconceptions recorded:

Notes for future teaching (areas for focus):

Specific children to follow up with:

2.3 Individual Background Knowledge Assessment

Name:

Unit of Study:

Observations/Questions:	Concept Awareness:

NOTES FOR FUTURE TEACHING:

Concepts to Learn:	Activities/Experiences to Teach Concepts:

2.4 Photograph Reflection Checklist: Preschool

Photograph's Contents:	Date(s):		
Reflection Questions		Yes	No
Are the children able to easily move through the room?			
Which centers are not being utilized?			
Does it appear that all the centers are providing enough materials for those visiting? Do any materials need to be updated or replaced?			
Are there any patterns in how children choose which centers to visit?			
Does it appear that children are able to focus on the given tasks?			
Does it appear that children are able to work collaboratively with the given space and materials?			
Are there any areas of the room that appear to have obstructed views due to furniture or other fixtures?			
Are the given center tasks addressing early learning standards?			

To-Do List	Plan to Complete

2.5 Photograph Reflection Checklist: Kindergarten and Early Elementary

Photograph's Contents:	Date(s):		
Reflection Questions		Yes	No
Are the children able to easily move through the room?			
Which centers are not being utilized?			
Does it appear that all the centers are providing enough materials for those visiting? Do any materials need to be updated or replaced?			
Are there any patterns in how children choose which centers to visit?			
Does it appear that children are able to focus on the given tasks?			
Does it appear that children are able to work collaboratively with the given space and materials?			
Are there any areas of the room that appear to have obstructed views due to furniture or other fixtures?			
Are the given center tasks addressing early learning standards?			
Does the center time structure appear to facilitate independent and small-group work?			
Does it appear that children are able to independently access the materials needed for their centers (independent or small-group work)?			
Are children working in small groups remaining on task?			
To-Do List	Plan to Complete		

From *Teaching in the Digital Age: Smart Tools for Age 3 to Grade 3* by Brian Puerling, © 2012.
Published by Redleaf Press, www.redleafpress.org. This page may be reproduced for classroom use only.

2.6 E-Photo Portfolio Goal-Setting Planner

Child:	Grade:
Marking Period:	Date:

Based on the photographs reviewed, skills exhibited include:

Based on the photographs reviewed, skills that need to be addressed include:

Activities/Experiences:	Dates:
1	
2	
3	

3

Rethinking Projectors

www.redleafpress.org/tech/3-1.aspx

After a long week, there are times when I enjoy a Friday night of getting comfortable on the couch and catching up on television shows I missed throughout the week or grabbing a dollar movie rental at the local Redbox. But if I reflect on why at times I choose to view a movie in a movie theater instead of renting the movie and watching it on a television screen, I think about the way the large screen captures my attention and draws me into the scene. I think of how the large screen brings the scene more vividly to life and heightens my senses. Watching *The Wizard of Oz* (1939), I can almost smell the poppies that put Dorothy to sleep; I can practically taste the salt water in *Cast Away* (2000); I can hear the loud, roaring winds of tornadoes in the movie *Twister* (1996); I can see breathtaking views of New York City in the film *Batman Returns* (1992); I can feel the heavy, wet rain on the islands while watching *Jurassic Park* (1993). Teachers can create these same experiences in the classroom to enhance learning. When teachers provide young children with the opportunity to activate their senses, they are able to understand, retain, and apply concepts.

"Hello, teachers, there is an overhead projector out in the first-floor hallway if anyone wants it." This was an e-mail sent to all teachers at the school

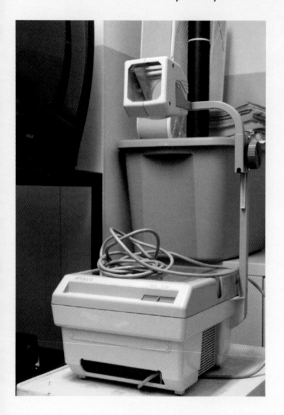

I was teaching at in the early fall of 2010. This line, though short and simple, depicts changes to classrooms in recent years. Fifteen years ago, overhead projectors could be found in classrooms throughout the United States. Now overhead projectors are a thing of the past. Gone are the days when teachers made document copies onto transparencies and had to purchase translucent manipulatives and dry-erase markers. In today's classrooms, LCD projectors and document cameras have revolutionized how teachers can engage children with skills and concepts.

Even though this new wave of projectors is making its way into classrooms, many teachers are unaware of the possibilities projectors have. Today's projectors provide authentic and meaningful experiences for learning. They provide teachers with the ability to capture the knowledge, learning, and engagement of young children. For example, a teacher can remotely take a photograph of a child's writing while the child projects and shares her writing with the class using an LCD projector and a document camera. Teachers can also use projectors (and other technology) to provide opportunities for young children to learn and practice observation skills in developmentally appropriate ways (Copple and Bredekamp 2009). Given the opportunity to carefully observe, children will naturally share what is familiar and ask questions about what is unfamiliar. When teachers use projectors effectively, the projectors have a rightful place in early childhood classrooms.

For example, an LCD projector, in conjunction with a document camera, such as an ELMO or IPEVO Point 2 View, can help a whole class engage in a read-aloud of a story. Document cameras provide the teacher with the ability to project "live" onto a large screen, whereas a traditional overhead projector casts shadows and will void anything that is not transparent. While reading a story using a document camera and LCD projector, you can pause at any moment and invite the class to pose any questions, observations, inferences, or predictions. The class can take a moment to look closely at the illustrations by zooming in with the zoom feature on these projectors. It's also easy to exhibit certain features in nonfiction text, such as charts, graphs, captions, and maps, or use a document camera to display an excerpt of a book or article that sparked particular interest or intrigue. In second or third grade, children learning how to write articles can observe a *National Geographic Kids* or *Time for Kids* magazine on the document camera and discuss common characteristics.

As depicted in the following examples, using projectors in the digital age typically requires other equipment in one of the three following combinations. Note that all of the strategies described in this chapter are achievable with these three combinations; however, preparing the equipment for the lesson will vary.

OPTION 1:

- LCD Projector
- Desktop/laptop computer
- Multi-touch mobile device with HDMI

This combination allows teachers to project documents, websites, videos, work samples, and photographs from a computer or multi-touch mobile device. Anything non-digital needs to be scanned and imported to the computer.

OPTION 2:

- LCD projector
- Document camera (ELMO or IPEVO Point 2 View, or similar)
- Desktop/laptop computer
- Multi-touch mobile device with HDMI

This combination allows teachers to project documents, websites, videos, work samples, photographs, multi-touch mobile devices, and 3-D objects with a high degree of flexibility. No scanning or importing of photographs or work samples is necessary with this option.

OPTION 3:

- LCD projector
- Interactive whiteboard (such as a SMART Board)
- Document camera
- Desktop/laptop computer
- Multi-touch mobile device with HDMI

This scenario easily allows teachers to project documents, websites, videos, work samples, photographs, and manipulative materials using the document camera. Connect the SMART Board to an LCD projector to create interactive activities with websites, videos, games, and digital books.

Using Projectors to Support Learning

Projectors offer children an opportunity to explore concepts in a variety of ways that are both interactive and engaging. When photographs, artwork, videos, student work, and math manipulatives are projected onto a large screen, they provide children with an opportunity to observe closely. Children become easily engaged in conversation over what they are observing and can become physically engaged if the screen is an interactive whiteboard. When used intentionally, projectors can become an important instructional tool to

- ✓ jump-start inquiry,

- ✓ support creativity,

- ✓ pursue inquiry concepts,

- ✓ dramatize stories,

- ✓ teach mathematics,

- ✓ share artwork and writing, and

- ✓ support academic learning with interactive whiteboards.

JUMP-START INQUIRY

Chapter 2 described a variety of ways to explore photographs, many of which can be used with projectors when it's important for a large group or the whole class of children to participate. When photographs are projected onto a large screen, children are able to engage with them in new ways. When images are projected, the learning experience becomes social in nature. When children are clustered in front of a large screen, they are given the opportunity to share with one another.

You can kick off an investigation of boats by projecting photographs of various types of boats. While doing so, you can invite the children to share questions or observations of what they are seeing. They can discuss events or moments in time when they have seen the boats in the photographs. You can gauge the children's background knowledge on certain concepts by asking questions that refer to the purposes of the types of boats or where people might find particular boats.

When young children are given the opportunity to observe, think, and share, they are able to process information in a variety of ways. They apply background knowledge to develop judgments and questions about what they are seeing. When children share their observations and questions, they learn that their peers can be a source for answers to their questions, and that others may share the same questions or observations.

When offering opportunities to share their questions and observations, you must consider development. Young children are naturally egocentric, so their ideas are important to them. One way to encourage and facilitate conversation is by utilizing a "turn and talk" strategy. I first learned about turn and talk several years ago while reading the second edition of *Strategies That Work: Teaching Comprehension for Understanding and Engagement* (Harvey and Goudvis 2007). Harvey and Goudvis recommend starting this practice in kindergarten; however, I have seen it be successful in many preschool classrooms as well. To use the turn and talk strategy, pose a question to the group and invite the children to turn to the person next to them to share their answers. This will take some practice and modeling. You will need to show the children what it looks like to share, listen, and respond. You will need to discuss the importance of taking turns while sharing. While the children share, glance over the group to see that they are discussing the question posed. You may consider joining pairs that may have trouble staying on task. After the children have shared their answers, invite children to share what they learned about their neighbors' ideas. Then ask them to share what they shared with their neighbor. This will help the children see the value in listening and understanding the other person's perspective and ideas.

When using this strategy with preschool children, explain the various definitions of the word *neighbor*. The first time I asked my class to turn and share with their neighbor, a child shouted out, "But Mr. Puerling, my neighbor isn't in this class!"

SUPPORT CREATIVITY

Observing photographs of novel experiences, cultures, and locations provides children with authentic experiences to build schema about these elements. Having this background knowledge helps children to become active participants in the development and use of a dramatic play center. In doing so, children can identify what jobs, roles, and rules are necessary for the center when it opens. Projecting photographs that depict real places and people can enhance this process if the photographs have a lot of detail.

When I was teaching about various ways to travel during an investigation of transportation, my preschool class wanted to create a space shuttle launch pad in our dramatic play center. To help the children determine what they would include in the launch pad, I projected photographs of a launch pad and the inside of a space shuttle. While viewing these photographs, the children were able to use a pointer to identify particular items that sparked interest or curiosity. Next, the class made observational drawings of what they saw in the photographs and what seemed important to include in the launch pad. Sketches were shared during a large-group activity, and a list was developed to guide the construction process. Being part of the planning and construction process deepened the children's understanding of the purpose of the center. This participation developed a sense of ownership and respect for the center.

In second-grade and third-grade classrooms, teachers may offer children the opportunity to develop skits in small groups in order to depict learning in a particular area. Children conducting these skits can project photographs as a backdrop to help set a stage or scene for audience members. In doing so, children can invite the audience into the learning they previously embarked upon. For example, a small group describing the first words of astronauts approaching the moon might project a photograph of a shuttle cockpit looking out into space. As the audience members listen to the children standing in front of the projected image, they can more authentically take the perspective of the astronauts who had the first glimpse of the moon.

Getting started using photographs and projectors in such a way can be fairly easy. There are a variety of ways to create a library of photographs for various topics and experiences. Consider reviewing your own personal collection of photographs to see if you have photographs that may be helpful. Using your own photographs will help the children connect to you and the content provided in the photographs. You may also consider asking the families of your students to search their albums for relevant photographs. Google and Yahoo images can also be a helpful resource for gathering photographs. Another option is to use books with colorful and vibrant photographs and place them under a document camera.

PURSUE INQUIRY CONCEPTS

During an inquiry study on Mexico, kindergarten teacher Kari Calabresa noticed that her students wanted to know if they ate the same foods as people who live in Mexico. To help her students learn about popular foods in Mexico, Kari projected a video clip showing traditional Mexican food and popular American versions of these foods. Note that Kari showed a video clip, not the entire video. Kari considered the age and development of these children. She knows that young children have a short attention span; therefore, she showed them the clip needed to answer the question rather than the whole video.

While the children watched this video clip, they recorded their questions and observations. Discussing the questions and observations after the video facilitated more conversation around the topic and provided an opportunity for Kari to gather information about the learning within the group.

DRAMATIZE STORIES

Teachers can create safe experiences for children to take the spotlight while adhering to the role of a familiar character from a story. Most young children love having the spotlight, but some children may be reluctant to take it. Children who are reluctant are often unsure about what to say or how to act in front of an audience, but providing a role that they know well helps them know how to act and present themselves in front of an audience. If you have a document camera, you can project any story. If you do not have a document camera, identify a simple but exciting story whose images are available electronically. Maurice Sendak's *Where the Wild Things Are* remains a popular children's book. When you type *Where the Wild Things Are* in to Google's search engine, several images from the story appear in the search results. Selecting one of these images to project onto a screen can set an enticing stage for children to act out the ferocious and exciting roles of the creatures of Max's imaginary world. Using projected images and other interactive theater systems allows children to bring their entire body into the story they are exploring (Yarosz 2007). When you add costumes to experiences like these, young children can visually and imaginatively try on the roles of others.

TEACH MATHEMATICS

Young children need concrete and hands-on learning experiences when exploring all early math skills within the five big ideas in mathematics: numbers and operations, measurement, geometry, algebraic concepts, and data analysis and probability (Copley 2000). Using a projector to illustrate concepts within the big ideas can help develop children's understanding and application. With an

LCD projector and a document camera, you can use pattern blocks to demonstrate a pattern that is easy to see and manipulate. After the children have developed an understanding of what is needed to create a pattern, they can use the projector to explore adding to, subtracting from, or creating their own patterns.

Projecting manipulatives and materials can support children's development of geometric skills and concepts. In order to develop skills related to shapes, a teacher can place various items of a similar shape under the document camera to identify similarities and differences between them. A teacher can also use a child's developing knowledge of geometric shapes to identify and develop patterns. Kindergarten teacher Lauren Cohen used a document camera to show her class how to create a shape-patterned caterpillar later in small groups. She created example patterns under the document camera with the exact materials the children would use. Projecting items in such a way helps children to visually see relationships between shapes and other items. Teachers need to carefully model how to use items in order for children to later explore with them with a particular focus.

SHARE ARTWORK AND WRITING

Developing self-confidence, a sense of creativity, and an ability to express through the arts are a few important skills learned in early childhood. You can support these skills by providing children with the opportunity to share and describe their artwork. How many times do children run up to teachers and parents and announce, "Look, look! Look at my picture. Do you like it?" You can harness this natural yearning in a way that provides a thoughtful framework for children to show and share. When children place their artwork on a document camera, they are able to share with a larger group or display their art in a unique format. In the sharing process, children are given the opportunity to share and celebrate their efforts. In this process, they are encouraged to convey their thoughts and describe the materials they used. They are encouraged to reflect and articulate the sequence of events it took to create their art. It is important to remember that very young children are developing the concept or script for what it means to share artwork or writing, so it may be helpful to have a list of questions or talking points to help the children through the sharing process.

You can also provide children with the opportunity to share their writing using projectors. When children share their writing, they are able to take the perspective of an author. Very young children can share what they tried writing and what is in the illustration they created, while children in second and third grade can describe their inspiration, the editing and revising process, the purpose of the writing, the audience for which it is intended, and their plan for future writing. This sharing takes a high level of metacognition, but it is necessary to continue the development of critical thinking and reflection skills. Keep in mind that not all children desire this type of attention. Use what you know about your class to determine who may be reluctant to share publicly. Chapter 4 includes a few strategies for how teachers can use audio recordings to support children who may be fearful of sharing.

SUPPORT ACADEMIC LEARNING WITH INTERACTIVE WHITEBOARDS

Interactive whiteboards, such as SMART Boards, provide children with an opportunity to physically engage with concepts (Preston and Mowbray 2008). Interactive whiteboards provide an active way to engage children with literacy concepts. In classrooms where children are learning the initial formation of letters, an interactive whiteboard can help children remember the unique formations of the letters. When children see letters the size of their bodies, they learn about them in a different way. Projecting items on a large screen offers the valuable experience of seeing things largely. In addition, when a group of children are clustered in front of an interactive whiteboard, they can discuss the similarities and differences between matched uppercase and lowercase letters with more social interaction as they move their bodies to draw and circle various similarities and differences. In kindergarten, a teacher can use an interactive whiteboard to help children develop the ability to isolate sounds in the beginning, middle, and end of words. After reading the book *The Letter Jj: Helping at School* by Hollie Endres (2005), you can use an interactive whiteboard to highlight the letter *J* and the sounds that go with it. You can then show a list of word cards on the screen that start with that sound and some that do not. After you show and read the list of word cards with the children, invite the children to touch and move the words into two groups: one group with words that begin with the *J* sound and a group of words that do not start with the *J* sound.

Children can be actively engaged in math activities as well by using interactive whiteboards. You can provide photographs of items from the community that portray shapes of varying sizes (for example, a stop sign, brick, sidewalk, window, stoplight, wheel, silo, trusses, column, or ball). Then ask the children to sort them into various groups, such as four-sided shapes, equal-sided shapes, or particular shapes such as triangles, cylinders, spheres, and so on. Children in first grade can create groups of coins equaling a particular amount by moving coins around on an interactive whiteboard. Children in second and third grade can move representations of sets to illustrate higher-level addition concepts. Research shows that first-grade children interacting with math skills using a SMART Board were more successful on tests assessing specific skills such as addition, time, and coin comparison and identification than children who did not use a SMART Board (Clemens, Moore, and Nelson 2001).

Sharon Godley, second grade teacher, describes how she uses SMART Boards, projectors, and software programs to introduce new Internet experiences to her class. (*www.redleafpress.org/tech/3-2.aspx*)

Children in first, second, or third grade can use interactive whiteboards to analyze data collected for an inquiry project. In a study on China, children worked to seek out an expert on the country to come for a visit. To find an expert, they conducted interviews of family members, friends, and peers in

Interactive whiteboards allow children to manipulate multimedia activities, watch videos, annotate images and photographs, and save notes and drawings for later review. Children are able to get up and use their whole body to draw letters, shapes, and numbers or move items around into groups. When children are provided with the opportunity to explore concepts while engaging their whole bodies, they activate and integrate the use of the several areas of their brains, such as their occipital lobes, to process what they are observing; their frontal lobes for information and thought processing; their temporal lobes for auditory and speech processing; and their motor bands for large-muscle movement (Woolfolk 2004). In doing so, children strengthen the connection between the hemispheres of their brains and the ability to recall and apply information in the future.

their school to see who had visited China or had knowledge of the country and culture. After collecting their data, the children organized their findings by creating a graph. The teacher then facilitated a social analysis of the collected data. The class observed the information collected together and determined which individuals to pursue for a possible visit.

Second- and third-grade teachers can also use interactive whiteboards in conjunction with interactive learning software such as DyKnow. DyKnow can be used in the classroom to manage learning experiences within laptop programs. Teachers participating in one-to-one laptop programs can use DyKnow to launch and close programs on all laptops using a single control computer. Interactive-learning software can be used to help introduce web-based programs used in literacy activities or science investigations.

Using Projectors to Support Documentation and Assessment

Teachers can use projectors in a variety of ways to gather valuable information about children's learning and development in a context that is authentic and embedded in classroom routines. The strategies provided here use projectors as a tool to elicit conversation and a child's knowledge, both of which can inform a teacher's instructional decisions. Teachers can use projectors to support assessment of

✓ knowledge at the end of an inquiry unit,

✓ children's observation of photographs and videos,

✓ writing development,

✓ learning experiences in mathematics, and

✓ articulation of an artist's or writer's process.

KNOWLEDGE AT THE END OF AN INQUIRY UNIT

Student teacher Jazmin Sanchez led a preschool class on an investigation of children around the world. In the investigation, the children learned about popular foods, games, and family activities. Jazmin wanted to create an experience to simultaneously assess and celebrate what the children learned throughout the investigation. Using Microsoft PowerPoint, she created a question-answer game appropriate for young children. With a combination of visual images and audio cues, the children were able to understand the answers and provide the correct questions. In creating this culminating activity, Jazmin wanted the children to see, hear, and remember what they had learned. She felt that the game she created was not only exciting for the preschoolers but also reaffirming as they were able to successfully demonstrate their knowledge over and over again. The use of the projector in this activity was essential as it preserved the social nature necessary to celebrate the conclusion of the unit. Jazmin hoped that the energy and excitement generated in the activity would propel the children into the next investigation. Under these larger objectives, other important literacy skills were being explored by the children, such as the ability to differentiate between questions and statements, the understanding of what a question mark represents while reading, and the ability to utilize language and new vocabulary to articulate thoughts and ideas and to address questions posed to them. It is evident that there are several layers of content within this activity that make this use of technology thoughtful and intentional. Interactive games like these and the use of other programs like Keynote and iMovie provide children with the opportunity not only to develop high-level literacy skills but also to develop technology skills (Parette et al. 2008). As children develop competencies with technology, they will begin to understand its relevance and usefulness in other contexts.

3.1 Photograph/Video Observation Reflection Sheet

Photograph/Video Collection:

Foods made in Mexico

Observations:	Questions:
"I have eaten that before." "My dad eats that." "That's my favorite kind of taco!" "I have eaten that at a restaurant once before."	"What is the green stuff on the chip?" "What is all the red stuff in the bowls around the chips?"

Future Activities/Learning Experiences:

Invite a chef or cook from a local Mexican restaurant to come in and talk about authentic Mexican foods. Explore similarities and differences with American foods.

3.2 Author's Share Reflection Sheet

Child: **Yara**   Grade: **2nd**   Date: **9/23/2011**

Title of Work: **My Summer Vacation: A Trip to Southern Illinois**

Observation of Skills

Skill/Concept:	Yes	No
Author and illustrator roles differentiated	X	
Illustrations match writing/dictation/oral description	X	
Attentive to and engages with audience		X
Sees self as author	X	
Feels comfortable sharing in front of others	X	

Skills within spelling development:
Has few spelling errors. Crosses words out when she spells them wrong and rewrites them correctly

Evidence:
Yara uses a dictionary to help herself find out how to spell words.

Other skills writer is attempting:
How to read her writing in ways that capture the attention of her audience

Evidence:
She reads with a low volume and appears frustrated when her audience cannot hear her voice.

Goals for future writing pieces:
Read with more inflection and louder volume to captivate audience attention.

Future activities or learning experiences to support goals:
First, listen to fluent readers using One More Story, an audio book in the listening center.

Later, have Yara record herself reading using a digital recording device and have her listen to herself read, paying attention to her inflection and enthusiasm.

CHILDREN'S OBSERVATION OF PHOTOGRAPHS AND VIDEOS

Photographs and videos are media for response and reflection. As teachers observe children observing photographs and videos—independently, in small groups, and in large groups—it's important to listen carefully to what children have to say. Use the Photograph/Video Observation Reflection Sheet (form 3.1) as a means to gather information about children's observations and questions. You can gather and analyze specific questions posed by children that will help inform future learning experiences, goals for individual children, identify gaps in background knowledge, and provide a general gauge for the enthusiasm for the content. When the Photograph/Video Observation Sheet is used over time, you can identify certain patterns or questions for particular children.

WRITING DEVELOPMENT

You can learn a significant amount from children when you listen closely to what children choose to share and how children share their own writing. You can learn specifics about early writing skills, spelling development, disposition toward writing, development of an identity as an author, ability to use language to articulate a process, and the use of new vocabulary. The Author's Share Reflection Sheet (form 3.2) provides a framework with which to observe and gather this valuable information as children share their writing. This form can help you develop individualized goals and learning experiences for specific children.

LEARNING EXPERIENCES IN MATHEMATICS

Teachers I know who use a projector to exhibit math concepts see the importance of providing experiences for all children to see and engage with manipulatives. They want to provide experiences for their class to come together to explore and learn about the wonders of mathematics. When you provide these experiences, you need to carefully observe how the children are receiving, understanding, and applying the new skill or concept. The Math Skill Reflection Sheet (form 3.3) provides a focused

3.3 Math Skill Reflection Sheet

Math Skill: Adding on to AB patterns		Date: 10/18/2011
Activity/Learning Experience: Using projector and document camera, teacher modeling how to create AB patterns with photographs of children in class. Then invite children to model adding onto pattern.		
Children's Interactions with Skill		Children
Observations: A majority of the children were able to model adding onto the patterns.		Deanna and Louise were unable to add onto the AB pattern twice.
Questions: "Ms. Perez, what would happen if we added another photo into the pattern?"		Kira
Possible Misconceptions: None at this time		
Future Activities/Learning Experiences: Conduct same activity and introduce ABC patterns Thomas	Kindergarten	Particular Children: Whole group, but pull Deanna and Louise for a quick review of AB pattern concept

way to assess a skill that has been taught and to evaluate the effectiveness of the learning experience by recording observations, questions, and potential misconceptions. If you don't have classroom assistants or volunteers to help complete the Math Skill Reflection Sheet, see the strategies in chapter 4 for how to use audio recordings to gather information for this assessment. Collecting data on each child's math skills in such a framework can help you monitor the progress of the children in your class and provide an opportunity to reflect on your instructional decision making.

ARTICULATION OF AN ARTIST'S OR WRITER'S PROCESS

Paula Denton (2007) and Peter Johnston (2004) have described the importance of crafting thoughtful and encouraging conversations around children's efforts. Young children seek the praise of adults. When you praise the work of children, you often miss the opportunity to encourage or nudge their development. When you acknowledge the efforts of children and then provide a task or question to extend their thought process, you help children develop a sense of intrinsic motivation. Consider this example of conversing with a child about his artwork while sharing it on a document camera with a projector.

Ms. Williams: Thomas, can you tell us what you drew?

Thomas: I drew my house and my yard.

Ms. Williams: Let's take a look at this picture. *(Selects a part of the picture to discuss.)* What is happening here? *(Looks for use of color.)* Can you tell us why you chose to use green right here?

Thomas: I was making grass, and I made my house here. I have never made a house like this one before.

Ms. Williams: Wow, you should be very proud of yourself, it looks like you spent a long time on this. Does anyone have any questions for Thomas?

Notice how Ms. Williams acknowledged the time and effort put into the picture. Also notice how she opened up the opportunity for Thomas to talk directly with his classmates by inviting them to ask him questions.

As you observe children talking to one another about their intentions and processes, you can learn all sorts of things about a child's ability to use language and vocabulary to articulate thoughts and ideas. You can learn about a child's ability to listen and respond. The Artwork/Writing Reflection Sheet (form 3.4) provides a framework for observing skill utilization while children are sharing their artwork or writing.

3.4 Artwork/Writing Reflection Sheet

Child: Thomas	Grade: Kindergarten	Date: 11/16/11

Title of Work: none given

Skill/Concept:	Yes	No
Sees self as an artist/author	X	
Able to describe materials used	X	
Attentive to and engages with audience	X	
Able to describe process to create piece	X	
Feels comfortable sharing in front of others	X	

Unique elements of creativity exhibited:

In this conversation with Thomas, I learned that he is acknowledging what he has and has not tried before. He appears to be excited about his success with trying something new.

Plan for next project:

Acknowledge this moment in a future experience to help nudge Thomas with a new or more sophisticated concept.

Future activities/learning experiences to harness creativity exhibited:

Next week when we are working in small groups with plant seeds, ask Thomas to consider the group leader role. This will be a new experience for him, but highlighting how good he felt when he tried creating a house like he did, he might be more likely to take on the challenge.

In Kate Herron's third-grade class, students use a document camera to share and discuss their postcard illustrations. (*www.redleafpress.org/tech/3-3.aspx*)

Using Projectors to Exhibit Learning

As I indicated in the opening of the chapter, large screens offer a way to invite an audience into what is occurring on and in front of the screen. Children can use projectors to articulate and support understanding of their ideas and processes.

Teachers can use projectors to exhibit

✓ artwork,

✓ work samples, and

✓ demonstrations.

ARTWORK

Children often feel pride in the creations they make. They take pride in their choice of materials and value the time spent in piecing together their creations. In order to showcase children's work, effort, and creativity, teachers can designate a daily featured artist. This daily featured artist can choose an item that she would like to share and add to the decoration of the classroom for the day. After she shares the artwork, the piece can be projected onto a designated bulletin board that recognizes and acknowledges the artist, title, and description of the creation. As indicated earlier, some children may be apprehensive to share publicly. Therefore, it is important to determine ways for all children to participate in the experience and handle any apprehension and fears sensitively.

WORK SAMPLES

When parents, guardians, and grandparents visit their child's school for open house or curriculum night, they come eager to see what their child has been busy doing at school. I remember bringing my parents to open house to show them where my desk was in the many rows across the room. I was also excited to show them where my work was hung up throughout the room. You can foster this same excitement with children and families by using a projector to exhibit children's artwork or writing. Depending on how the night is structured, you can create a short video consisting of work samples. If the night is structured into short sessions, rotate the children's projected work samples and discuss particular skills and concepts being explored in the classroom.

DEMONSTRATIONS

In second and third grade, children are developing refined skills in particular interest areas. In areas of study such as foods from around the world, children can exhibit their knowledge of how to prepare foods from various cultures. In order to do this, children can present needed ingredients under the document camera. They can also use the document camera to demonstrate how to prepare and mix certain ingredients.

In an art class, a teacher can place prints under a document camera and invite students to demonstrate how to employ new critique strategies. The document camera provides children with an opportunity to all get the same view of the print and easily move between prints.

In preschool and kindergarten classrooms, a document camera can be used to invite children to demonstrate how their peers can use certain materials. They can model how to use chain links to create chains of varying lengths. When the chain links are under the camera and projected on the screen, the children have a better visual of how many links are in each chain being modeled.

◆　　◆　　◆

Projectors add an important experience to early childhood classrooms. They provide children with opportunities to engage their senses in exploring new and higher-level concepts. Whether items are projected on a screen or moved around on an interactive whiteboard, these experiences invite children to make the learning experience individualized and meaningful.

PLACING YOUR PROJECTOR

Teachers are constantly faced with a multitude of obstacles that make it difficult to implement new practices in their classrooms. Many teachers cite a lack of time and space as issues in their classroom. In times like these, teachers often utilize spaces in their classroom that have multiple functions. When I acquired a projector for my classroom, I was faced with the issue of where to put it. Most classrooms in the school where I was teaching were using projectors but had them in a stationary place in the classroom. I spoke with a first-grade teacher, and she showed me how she had positioned the cables underneath a meeting rug to make her station work. I spoke to a kindergarten teacher who described how the stationary spot worked for her class. As a preschool teacher of three- to five-year-old children, I felt that a stationary spot was not the best utilization of space for my classroom, as they need to utilize that space to move around the classroom. Also, very young children are still developing motor control, so to avoid damaging equipment, I felt it best to have it out of the children's way. One night

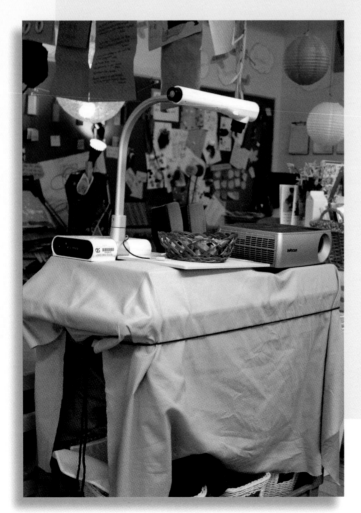

after everyone had left, I took a look around my classroom, wondering if there were any nontraditional items I could use to house a mobile technology cart. I noticed a storage cart in a corner of my room that I had once used to transport lunches to my classroom from the cafeteria. That year, I had several children bring lunches from home rather than eating school lunches, which freed up the cart. I decided to turn the storage cart into our classroom technology cart.

The cart offered the space to house and use the speakers, laptop, LCD projector, ELMO, and iPad at any time. Having all these items organized on a cart reduced setup time to almost no time at all. The station shown in the photo requires literally no setup time at all for kindergarten through third-grade teachers, since all the equipment is accessible at any time.

In getting a technology space set up in your classroom, it is important to ask yourself these questions:

- What equipment do I currently have?

- What equipment do I hope to obtain?

- What spaces or centers do I need in my classroom?

- Do I want the technology space to be stationary or mobile?

- What is my budget for furniture?

- What is my budget for technology equipment?

- How can classroom assistants, other professionals, parent volunteers, or older children be helpful in the organization of this space?

It is important to consider the answers to all these questions to most thoughtfully plan out this space. The answers to these questions will be helpful in determining how you go about developing a technology space in your classroom.

Forms

3.1 Photograph/Video Observation Reflection Sheet

www.redleafpress.org/tech/3-1.pdf

3.2 Author's Share Reflection Sheet

www.redleafpress.org/tech/3-2.pdf

3.3 Math Skill Reflection Sheet

www.redleafpress.org/tech/3-3.pdf

3.4 Artwork/Writing Reflection Sheet

www.redleafpress.org/tech/3-4.pdf

3.1 Photograph/Video Observation Reflection Sheet

Photograph/Video Collection:

Observations:	Questions:

Future Activities/Learning Experiences:

3.2 Author's Share Reflection Sheet

Child:	Grade:	Date:

Title of Work:

Observation of Skills

Skill/Concept:	Yes	No
Author and illustrator roles differentiated		
Illustrations match writing/dictation/oral description		
Attentive to and engages with audience		
Sees self as author		
Feels comfortable sharing in front of others		

Skills within spelling development:

Evidence:

Other skills writer is attempting:

Evidence:

Goals for future writing pieces:

Future activities or learning experiences to support goals:

3.3 Math Skill Reflection Sheet

Math Skill:	Date:

Activity/Learning Experience:

Children's Interactions with Skill	Children
Observations:	
Questions:	
Possible Misconceptions:	
Future Activities/Learning Experiences:	Particular Children:

3.4 Artwork/Writing Reflection Sheet

Child:	Grade:	Date:

Title of Work:

Skill/Concept:	Yes	No
Sees self as an artist/author		
Able to describe materials used		
Attentive to and engages with audience		
Able to describe process to create piece		
Feels comfortable sharing in front of others		

Unique elements of creativity exhibited:

Plan for next project:

Future activities/learning experiences to harness creativity exhibited:

4 Using Audio Recordings to Capture Powerful Moments

www.redleafpress.org/tech/4-1.aspx

When I taught preschool, each morning we started our day off with a song that greeted everyone. The song included everyone's name at one point or another. In planning an end-of-the-year DVD, I wanted to include this song in the video I was going to create. In order to do that, I needed to record the song as we sang. I told my class that we were going to use our song in a movie I was working on, and we needed to sing our best so that families and friends could hear what great singers we were when they watched the video. We recorded the song several times over a few days, each time listening to see if it was our best yet. In this experience, the children listened together and used what they had learned with their music teacher to judge whether it was their best work. In the end, we had a well-sung version recorded that was included in the end-of-the-year video.

Capturing a moment in time with an audio recording device provides an amazing opportunity to revisit and relive important events or conversations. When teachers

95

record conversations or moments, they are able to explore children's learning, social skills, and language. It's valuable to be able to listen and relisten with a critical ear to learn valuable information about a child's progress and development. Collecting audio recordings also provides a powerful tool to encourage reflection and collaboration with families, other educators, and other professionals. In this chapter, audio recording devices refer to any of the following:

- digital voice recorders (DVR)

- MP3 players with audio recording capabilities

- iPods with audio recording capabilities or attachable microphone

- iPads or other tablets

- smartphones with audio recording capabilities

- SmartPen

Using Audio Recordings to Support Learning

Audio recordings can be gathered and utilized in a whole host of ways. They provide children and teachers with an opportunity to revisit classroom experiences to learn more about what is being explored. Strategies for gathering and using audio recordings can be easily implemented in classroom routines and used to

- ✓ create messages for others,

- ✓ capture conversations with classroom guests,

- ✓ organize a listening center,

- ✓ enhance a listening center,

- ✓ develop classroom community,

- ✓ facilitate skill development in music, and

- ✓ support development of reading fluency.

CREATE MESSAGES FOR OTHERS

Young children are building a capacity to respect the needs, wants, and materials of themselves and others. It's important to keep this fact in the forefront of your mind while planning and introducing new materials and experiences to children. When I was teaching preschool, the class determined that we were going to get a fish for the classroom. The science center was transformed into a research center where children could browse brochures and photographs to learn facts about fish. Picture and nonfiction books on freshwater and tropical fish were available to help the children learn about fish that might or might not be appropriate for our classroom. An iPad was available with an application that showed several types of fish found in waters across the globe. A research folder was available for children to store any observational drawings and ideas.

After deciding which fish to purchase, we discussed the importance of welcoming guests, visitors, and new members to our classroom. I asked the

children to come up with a way to help welcome the fish to the classroom. They came up with several ideas, such as voting on a possible name, setting up the aquarium, finding a special spot in the classroom for a home, and creating welcome messages to give to the fish. Given the varying ability and skill levels, a variety of materials were put out for the children to create their welcome messages. Along with paper, markers, colored pencils, and crayons to create messages, there was also an iPad to capture oral welcome messages. Some children drew pictures of particular centers in the classroom in attempts to help acquaint the fish with the physical space, while other children drew illustrations of children looking at books and lining up to go outside to help the fish become acquainted with the routines of the classroom. Children who recorded welcome messages spoke about their hopes for a comfortable new home. In a welcome celebration for the arrival of our fish, we circled up in the reading corner to give the children an opportunity to share their welcome messages.

I pulled our technology cart to the area and hooked up our iPad to speakers to listen to the recorded welcome messages. As the children took part in the welcoming of the fish to the classroom, they had to recall the purposes of the many materials and routines put in place. Notice how the audio recording of the welcome messages was a small piece of a large goal to further develop the idea of respect, care, and knowledge of classroom materials and routines. The use of technology was a single experience among many ways to contribute to the understanding of a particular concept. In this experience, recording the welcome notes provided an opportunity for the children to express their knowledge in a fashion that was respectful of their development and learning style; for example, orally recording messages gave children with very early writing and drawing skills a chance to independently share their thoughts and ideas too. The whole experience also provided me with ways to assess each child's skill development in a variety of areas.

CAPTURE CONVERSATIONS WITH CLASSROOM GUESTS

When teachers utilize an inquiry-based approach to curriculum in early childhood classrooms, the resources used to support learning are key. Oftentimes, some of the most authentic and informative resources are individuals who have a significant amount of information to offer on a particular area in an investigation. In a kindergarten classroom embarking on an investigation of sea animals, a likely expert to support the students' research may be a caretaker at a zoo or aquarium. In a first-grade classroom investigating American Indian tribes, a likely expert may be an individual with an American Indian tribal background or an American Indian museum tour guide. For third-grade students learning about their city or community, a potential expert might include an alderman, city council representative, or perhaps a mayor.

When these individuals visit an early childhood classroom, typically the children's excitement is through the roof. This excitement may be overwhelming for some children, and therefore some children may miss some of the content shared during the visit. Given this, and the natural need for multiple experiences with content and concepts, recording the conversations with these visitors can provide teachers and the children with the ability to revisit particular parts of the visit with accuracy. Revisiting these moments will also furnish additional experiences with the guest and the content provided within the conversation.

ORGANIZE A LISTENING CENTER

Sheri Burkeen, an early childhood technology coordinator at St. Mary's Episcopal School in Memphis, Tennessee, was approached by one of the junior kindergarten teachers. The teacher was inquiring about obtaining an iPod Touch to replace the CD player in her listening center. The school purchased forty iPod Touches to help streamline the organization of the listening centers throughout the classrooms. Now, several children can listen to a single audiobook anywhere in the classroom.

Teachers who use an iPod or an iPod Touch to organize their audiobooks are able to preserve audio files much more easily. Purchasing audio files is also less expensive than purchasing a CD of a single book. In order to manage students using an iPod or iPod Touch to listen to audiobooks, some teachers have created a special classroom assistant—a child who is an expert in using the device. When other children need assistance finding a particular book on the device, they can first ask the peer expert. As Sheri and her team began using their iPod Touches in classrooms, they quickly learned many possibilities for how the

Snow had fallen during the night.
It covered everything as far as he could see.

devices could be used to support learning. They soon learned what an amazing device they had to share between their classrooms. (Additional strategies for multi-touch mobile devices are provided in chapter 8.)

ENHANCE A LISTENING CENTER

Traditionally, a listening center has been used to support literacy development while children listen to audio-books and follow along. Additional ways to support the development of literacy skills in a listening center include listening to music, conversing with classroom guests, and doing activities with enrichment teachers. The website One More Story (www.onemorestory.com), 2011 winner of *Learning* magazine's Teachers' Choice Award, is a resource that allows children to virtually engage with popular children's literature. With a purchased school or home subscription, children can access a substantial library of books. This website provides children with an opportunity to engage with literature in ways that activate auditory and visual senses (Roskos, Brueck, and Widman 2009). As shown in the One More Story screenshot *Snowy Day*, a child can listen to the story while the program highlights the words being read aloud. You can change the settings to make the literature experience most appropriate and meaningful for individual children.

A listening center essentially is intended to activate and focus a child's sense of hearing to engage with concepts. Considering this, a listening center can support other disciplines just as well as it supports literacy. Recordings of conversations with classroom guests can be placed in a listening center to support science, social studies, social skills, and math concepts. As the children listen to these conversations multiple times, they become more familiar with the content, the guest, and how these visits will work and support investigations in the future. As the children listen to the conversations, they are given additional opportunities to think about the content, which can lead to more questions to propel the investigation into deeper areas.

DEVELOP CLASSROOM COMMUNITY

Teachers serve children who are members of different cultures, family structures, and income levels. In families where parents or guardians are working long hours, finding ways to become directly involved in their children's classrooms can be difficult. It is the responsibility of both the teachers and the families to identify ways for individuals to be involved in the classroom. Teachers can help families contribute to the classroom electronically by sending home a digital voice-recording device with a book from the classroom. At home, the families can record the story while reading it. Then you can place the book and the recording of the reading in the listening center when they are returned. Inviting families to

participate in experiences such as this provides them with an opportunity to contribute to the literacy development of the class and the overall community as children learn how other families engage with and enjoy literature.

FACILITATE SKILL DEVELOPMENT IN MUSIC

Music teachers carefully create learning experiences to help children develop a whole host of skills related to listening to and matching tones and pitches. To support the development of these skills, teachers can collaborate with music teachers to identify particular skills that need further development. After identifying these skills, the classroom teacher can record the students as they work on the identified skills and singing-related experiences that the music teacher has planned and provided the class. For example, a classroom teacher and a music teacher collaborate to identify that the students need to focus on the ability to identify the difference between sounds considered piano (soft) and those considered forte (loud). The classroom teacher may record an activity facilitated by the music teacher in which the music teacher explores the differences between piano and forte. Later, the classroom teacher can facilitate a similar activity to support the development of the skill and/or she can place the recording in a listening center for the children to revisit the experience independently or in a small group. When the music teacher returns, the class will have had additional experiences to develop the skill, thus preparing them for the next experience in the learning sequence.

Kari Calabresa, kindergarten teacher, describes how children use multi-touch mobile devices to record their own reading to support their development of reading fluency. (*www.redleafpress.org/tech/4-2.aspx*)

SUPPORT DEVELOPMENT OF READING FLUENCY

Elementary teachers can use an iPod or iPod Touch with a digital voice-recording application to help children select a just-right book. After choosing a book, the children can record themselves reading the book aloud. Afterward, they can use headphones to listen to their recording. As children

listen to themselves reading the story, they can evaluate whether they read too quickly or too slowly. While following along in the book, they can determine whether they skipped any words or lines. Later, you can listen to these readings to determine skills and strategies children are using independently.

Using Audio Recordings to Support Assessment

As demonstrated in the learning strategies, audio recordings offer opportunities to revisit previous events. Revisiting important moments allows teachers to gather information on children's progress and development. With the opportunity to pause, rewind, and listen again, teachers can critically reflect on a child's processing.

Teachers also can use audio recordings to assess

✓ oral retelling of stories,

✓ reading,

✓ understanding and levels of inquiry, and

✓ understanding and misconceptions in science experiments.

ORAL RETELLING OF STORIES

Some teachers utilize curricular or literacy approaches that include multiple readings of a single book. When teachers approach literature with a multiple read-aloud model, by the end of the experience series, children are typically familiar enough to retell the story. Audio recordings can support the development of story retelling. Diane Salk, a teacher of three- to six-year-old children in Chicago, includes retelling stories as an option during a self-selected center period of the day. While the children orally retell a story, Diane records them using a digital voice recorder. She then replays the storytellings to the children and uses the recordings to focus on assessment after the children have gone home. Teachers of children not yet reading can use the Oral Retelling Checklist (form 4.1) to explore the various prereading skills children exhibit.

4.1 Oral Retelling Checklist

Name: Griselle Date: 12/5/2011

Book: Yoko Writes Her Name
Author: Rosemary Wells

Skill:	Observed	Not Observed	N/A
Referred to the title of the story.	X		
Referred to the author of the story.		X	
Referred to most characters.	X		
Referred to main events in the story.	X		
Referred to problem in the story.	X		
Used inflection/enthusiasm.	X		
Maintained story-event sequence.	X		
Used inflection/enthusiasm.	X		

Notes for Future Learning Experiences:

In future read alouds with the class, discuss the author more explicitly. Talk about the author's role, work, and effort in writing a book.

READING

Similarly, teachers of children who can read independently can use the Read-Aloud Checklist (form 4.2) to explore decoding skills and ability to sight-read words. While using this checklist, teachers can gain a sense of what skills a child demonstrates. This checklist will also help teachers understand a child's ability to monitor his or her reading. You can listen to how a child reads, paying attention to the use of appropriate inflection. While listening to a child orally reading sentences, you can hear how an inflection varies between questions and statements.

UNDERSTANDING AND LEVELS OF INQUIRY

Teachers can use audio recording devices to capture children's conversations around a particular task, then review them later to determine the direction of inquiry, identify misunderstandings and questions, and determine how children are or are not understanding material. The Small-Group Recording Reflection Sheet (form 4.3) can be used to review small-group recordings and gather valuable information about particular children or groups. The information gathered

4.2 Read-Aloud Checklist

| Name: Maggie | | Date: 9/16/2011 | | |

Book: Snip Snap! What's That?
Author: Mara Bergman

Skill	Observed	Not Observed	N/A
Referred to the title of the story.	X		
Referred to the author of the story.	X		
Read words on the page rather than made up words to match illustrations.	X		
Read familiar sight words.	X		
Used familiar letter sounds to sound out unfamiliar words.	X		
Reread sentence after decoding a word.	X		
Did not skip pages.	X		
Did not skip words.	X		
Used inflection/enthusiasm.	X		
Read "!" and "?" with appropriate inflection.	X		

Notes for Future Learning Experiences:

Reread this story with Maggie and acknowledge the exclamation points. Discuss the difference in how readers will sound when reading sentences that end in a period, question mark, or exclamation point. Have her reread the second half of the story after I have modeled reading sentences with exclamation points with inflection and enthusiasm.

4.3 Small-Group Recording Reflection Sheet

| Children in Group: Barbara, Bianca, and Catherine | Date: 4/15/11 |

Unit of Study/Investigation:
Fantasy stories

Group Activity Objective:
Create a short story collaboratively.

Group Activity:
In a small group, create a fiction story using imaginary characters.

Small-Group Conversation Content

Observations posed during activity

The three girls were easily able to create a fiction story with a setting and basic plot including a problem and solution.

Barbara took a comfortable leadership role in developing the story.

Questions posed during activity

"I wonder how we can end this story."

"I wonder what should happen next to keep the story exciting."

Possible misunderstandings

None at this time.

Many basic DVRs sold today offer the ability to create multiple folders with which to house and organize recordings. These folders could correspond with groups in your class or particular learning experiences. Recorders with the ability to plug into a computer with a USB port offer teachers the ability to import recordings easily and organize folders for individual children. I recommend that teachers working with younger children maintain control of the recorder for most purposes; however, children as young as five years old can begin making their own recordings. You should exercise careful modeling as you begin to invite the children to make their own recordings.

can be used to steer future investigations, review content previously covered in the investigation, or identify children who need help with specific skills or concepts.

Audio recording pens, such as the SmartPen, can also be used to capture conversations in small groups. Audio recording pens provide teachers with a device that can capture valuable information in two ways. A SmartPen collects audio recordings and provides a written dictation of the recording. As you use the pen to dictate a child's words, you can audio-record the conversation. Later, the pen can be plugged into a computer to review the dictation. While reviewing, you can listen to the recordings and watch notes be rewritten on the screen. Some teachers have used a SmartPen to record children's storytelling. There are particular times when it is appropriate to be done individually, in a small

group, or in a large group. If a child is somewhat reluctant to speak or share in front of others, it is more than likely that working with that child individually would be the best circumstance to elicit ideas. If you have social and literacy goals for particular children, recording their stories in a small group might be best, as the children will need to work together to develop a plan for the basic elements of a simple story. When you want to strengthen the community fabric of the classroom, recording stories in a large group allows the entire class to be part of the process and the product.

Preschool children use SmartPens to support their writing and reading development. (*www.redleafpress.org/tech/4-3.aspx*)

UNDERSTANDING AND MISCONCEPTIONS IN SCIENCE EXPERIENCES

Young children come to classrooms with varied experiences and differing banks of background knowledge. These variances can become particularly evident when you are introducing new concepts in science. When taking children on a journey and exploration of science concepts, you will find audio recording devices helpful to monitor children's observations, questions, misconceptions, and understanding. If a preschool class investigation includes learning vocabulary to describe differences between items, new and appropriate terms may include *light, tall, short, wide, skinny, narrow, flat, bumpy, rough,* and *smooth*. To encourage children to use these new terms, a teacher can ask a small group of children to describe how items in a basket are the same and different. Using an audio recording device frees the teacher to ask questions and make observations to extend children's thinking and language. You do not need to take notes, as the recorder captures all the responses of all the children. Later, while reviewing the recording, the teacher can use the Small-Group Recording Reflection Sheet (form 4.3) to gather information on the children's observations, questions, understandings, and possible misconceptions.

Audio Recordings to Exhibit Learning

Families often want to know what is happening throughout the learning day. Teachers can use audio recordings in a variety of ways to revisit moments in time to discuss progress and development, celebrate work and effort, and share information to educate families on early childhood and child development. Specific strategies include using audio recordings to

✓ publish class songs,

✓ publish audiobooks, and

✓ create a visitors' listening center.

As children publish songs, books, and audio recordings, they learn the various publication processes for the different pieces of work. Within the layers of the these publication processes, it is important to be cognizant of the multitude of other social, math, literacy, language, and technology skills children learn. They learn how to communicate their opinions as they negotiate and decide how they will publish their work. They will have to decide how many posters to create for the classroom and school to effectively advertise the release of their work. They learn the power of words and illustrations as they send messages to family and friends. They learn to use new vocabulary specific to certain ways of publishing. They also learn authentic ways to utilize the Internet and other technological devices in our daily lives. Chapter 6 explores additional ways to present and publish children's work and effort.

PUBLISH CLASS SONGS

A high-quality early childhood literacy program includes experiences in which children learn about how their work can be published. When teachers describe publication as a way of celebrating hard work and achievement, children are better able to connect with the concept. Once children understand this basic idea of publication, teachers can easily transfer to the more complex ideas of publishing. Within the conversations about publishing, it is important to discuss how publication is not only about writing. Consider these examples to discuss various opportunities for publishing.

OCCUPATION	PUBLICATION
Author	book/e-book/digital books/audiobook
Illustrator	book/magazine/newspaper illustrations
Artist	paintings/sculptures/gallery showings
Singer/performer	stage performance/record songs
Researcher/scientist	articles

When children are aware of the many ways to publish work, you can use audio recordings to publish their work. Electronic music stores, such as iTunes, allow you to access music anywhere you have an Internet connection. Taking children on a brief tour of the iTunes music store can help them not only understand how their friends and family access music but also develop a deeper understanding of how music can be published and shared with people around the world. Afterward, you can help your class decide on a song to publish through recording and sharing on a classroom website for families and friends to listen to. After recording the song and having the children confirm that it represents their hardest work and effort, it is important to celebrate publication. Celebrating could include choosing a date on a calendar for when the song will be available online and posting class-created advertisements throughout the classroom and school. It could also include a class-made e-mail announcement sent to students' friends and family with a link to the uploaded recording. A release party is another way to celebrate the publishing of the song. This party could include invitations to family and friends, a live performance of the song, and photo opportunities for the singers and their family and friends.

PUBLISH AUDIOBOOKS

Authors can publish their work through printed books, e-books, and audiobooks. To help children learn what these look like and how people use them, it's important to offer children the opportunity to try publishing their own work in these fashions. For example, after a child has written a book, he can publish his book further by creating an audiobook. With the help of a teacher or classroom volunteer, a child can record herself reading the book.

It's fun to celebrate the release of children's audiobooks. Create a "Recent Audiobook Releases" poster for the listening center to advertise the names of the authors and titles. This can help young authors develop confidence and pride in their work. Other ways to celebrate the release of audiobooks include having a public sharing of an audiobook with an announcement of its inclusion in the classroom listening center. Once this has been done, the audio file and book can be added to the listening center for other children or classroom visitors to enjoy. The celebration component is key to the publication of children's work. It values the hard work and effort children have invested and will more than likely encourage children to try new things in the future.

CREATE A VISITORS' LISTENING CENTER

As indicated earlier, a listening center does not necessarily have to focus only on literacy skills. In fact, visitors can participate in a listening center that exhibits how and what children learn. Some families, colleagues, and administrators are unaware of how and what children learn in various centers or classroom experiences. It is important

to advocate for developmentally appropriate practices by sharing how experiences in your classroom will benefit children next year rather than tomorrow. For example, when preschool children engage with literature and concepts through dramatic play, they develop important skills. As they negotiate roles, determine a plot, and listen to other children's ideas, they put their own needs and wants on hold. Over time, they develop the ability to take turns. These experiences support children's overall cognitive development (Copple and Bredekamp 2009, Riley et al. 2008). When they take on roles, children develop self-regulation. When they create a story line, children learn how to organize story events into beginning, middle, and end sequences, a skill that will later help them write stories with events that occur in a logical sequence. Items like these are important for families, colleagues, and administrators to be aware of. Creating a visitors' listening center outside of a classroom or somewhere in the school can help educate others. In a visitors' listening center, it's helpful to include photographs of children at work in the particular center or an experience, along with statements of early childhood goals or standards that are being addressed in the photographs.

Children's work samples can also be included with reflection notes from the teacher indicating the skills a particular child is exhibiting. Excerpts from professional literature advocating for these practices can also help develop support. In conjunction with these visual representations, the audio recordings of children's conversations help visitors connect the children's choices to the concepts and the learning that is occurring. For example, if you were to develop a visitors' listening center exploring what the children are learning in a grocery store dramatic play center, you might highlight some basic skills exhibited in the center, such as taking turns, counting objects, asking questions, responding to questions, and making observations. To illustrate some of these skills, provide an audio recording from the center with a conversation exchange such as the following:

Paul: You be the cashier, and I will be the customer.

Alex: No, I want to be the customer first, you can be it second.

Paul: Okay, you can be first this time. Next time, I will be first.

Alex: Okay.

Paul: Okay, I want to buy these things: a can of pears, some cereal, milk, and this soy sauce.

Alex: How many things do you have?

Paul: Um, one, two, three, four. I have four things.

To help illustrate the skills these two boys are exhibiting, it's helpful to include a few reflection notes such as the following:

> Paul and Alex worked together to create a plan for who will be the customer first and second. Alex wanted to be the customer first, but he decided to give Paul the opportunity to be the customer first. Alex asked Paul a question, and Paul responded. Notice how Paul counted his items from one through four and stated the full number of items he had in his group. Paul is currently working on his one-to-one correspondence and labeling sets.

In providing these reflections, you can further interpret the recording for listeners. After reading the reflection, listeners can more clearly see what skills children utilize while engaged in dramatic play.

◆　◆　◆

Audio recordings provide teachers with the opportunity to time travel. A teacher's day is full of paperwork, conversations, thoughts, questions, and to-do lists. At the end of the day, it can be difficult to remember what children said throughout the day to accurately record for assessment purposes. Audio recording devices can capture all of what children say and allow you to sit down and immerse yourself in their language and conversation. Audio recordings also provide you with valuable information to share with family members and other professionals to best support children. Audio recordings can also be used in amazing ways to celebrate learning and effort to share with other children, families, and the community.

» TOOLBOX TIP

MOVING INTO AUDIO RECORDINGS

If you are interested in using an audio recording device but do not have one, before purchasing one, discuss your intention with friends and family. As technology changes quickly, so must people; therefore, a friend or family member might have one of the items listed in the beginning of the chapter. When you are ready to purchase one or more audio recording devices for your classroom, it is important to consider the following questions to identify the best recording device to purchase.

- What will you use it for?
- Who will use it?
- How often will it be used?
- Do you want to be able to organize your audio files into folders on the device?
- Do you want to be able to plug it into a computer to transfer, organize, and manipulate the audio files?
- Do you want the device to have other functions?
- Do you want the ability to hook up a microphone to the device?

Thinking carefully about these questions will help an associate at an electronics store assist you in making the best purchase for your needs.

Forms

④

4.1 Oral Retelling Checklist

www.redleafpress.org/tech/4-1.pdf

4.2 Read-Aloud Checklist

www.redleafpress.org/tech/4-2.pdf

4.3 Small-Group Recording Reflection Sheet

www.redleafpress.org/tech/4-3.pdf

4.1 Oral Retelling Checklist

Name:

Date:

Book:

Author:

Skill:	Observed	Not Observed	N/A
Referred to the title of the story.			
Referred to the author of the story.			
Referred to most characters.			
Referred to main events in the story.			
Referred to problem in the story.			
Used inflection/enthusiasm.			
Maintained story-event sequence.			
Used inflection/enthusiasm.			

Notes for Future Learning Experiences:

4.2 Read-Aloud Checklist

Name:

Date:

Book:

Author:

Skill:	Observed	Not Observed	N/A
Referred to the title of the story.			
Referred to the author of the story.			
Read words on the page rather than made up words to match illustrations.			
Read familiar sight words.			
Used familiar letter sounds to sound out unfamiliar words.			
Reread sentence after decoding a word.			
Did not skip pages.			
Did not skip words.			
Used inflection/enthusiasm.			
Read "!" and "?" with appropriate inflection.			

Notes for Future Learning Experiences:

4.3 Small-Group Recording Reflection Sheet

Children in Group:	Date:

Unit of Study/Investigation:

Group Activity Objective:

Group Activity:

Small-Group Conversation Content

Observations posed during activity

Questions posed during activity

Possible misunderstandings

5

Expanding the Classroom with Videoconferencing and Webcams

www.redleafpress.org/tech/5-1.aspx

Preschool teacher Rachel Kennedy and her assistant, Jennifer Berg-Wallish, discussed how they were going to handle Jennifer's trip to see her grandson in the opening weeks of school. Both Rachel and Jennifer value all efforts, big and small, to develop classroom community. In order to make sure the children in their class remained connected to Jennifer during her trip to New York, they planned a time to use Skype to visit with Jennifer. While the children were at an enrichment class, Rachel set up her computer with the classroom SMART Board and got connected with Jennifer before the children walked in. Once the children walked in, they saw Jennifer projected on the screen. As the children walked in and slowly sat down on the rug, Jennifer began greeting the children. The look on the children's face was priceless, a mixture of excitement and confusion. They were clearly excited to see Jennifer but were confused as to how she could see them if she was not present in the classroom. Rachel and Jennifer explained how the setup worked and then got busy catching up. The children shared what art projects they had been working on and what songs they had been singing. Jennifer shared how her grandson had also started school. The children were able to ask her questions about where she was staying, like "What's the weather like there?" and "Where are you sleeping while you are there?"

It is important to remember that the classroom is a concept rather than a space within walls. As new schools are built and older schools are updated, technology is incorporated in a variety of ways. Plans may include small meeting spaces in commons areas, a recording studio, or sophisticated science laboratories. Classrooms may have interactive whiteboards, projectors, document cameras, and flat-screen televisions. With these technologies, teachers can invite people to participate in the classroom experience without requiring guests to actually enter the classroom. Webcams and videoconferencing programs, such as Skype and iChat, can help teachers provide meaningful and authentic experiences for children to engage with content. Classrooms adhering to an inquiry-based approach to content and curriculum see the value in providing children with hands-on experiences to explore, ask, discuss, and reflect. Within these experiences, experts in a particular area are brought into classrooms to help guide children to deeper understanding and further inquiry. Teachers searching for experts often come across obstacles like availability and scheduling. Using webcams and videoconferencing programs can help circumvent these common obstacles. When experts are not available because of distance, videoconferencing programs provide an opportunity to still engage with the individual without his having to travel. Additionally, if expert-appearance fees are beyond the reach of a school or program, videoconferencing opportunities may be available at a lower cost.

Today, standard Apple and PC desktop and laptop computers are equipped with built-in, high-quality webcams. If you have an older computer without a webcam, you can purchase a webcam to use with your current computer, as long as you have an Internet connection. There are several things to consider when determining the best webcam. It is important to identify a budget, the intended frequency of use, the age and current condition of the computer to be used with the webcam, and the quality of video you want to achieve. Use the Choosing a Webcam Toolbox Tip to help identify elements needed in a webcam. Completing and bringing this guide to an electronics store will help an employee understand what you need and value in a webcam.

» TOOLBOX TIPS

CHOOSING A WEBCAM

It is important to be thoughtful about the webcam you choose for your setting. Consider your goals, your budget, and other equipment necessary to carry out experiences. Use these questions to help you in your search for the webcam that best fits your setting.

- What operating system is most used in your school or classroom?
- Do you have a computer that can be used to host webcam and videoconferencing experiences?

    If no, is there one available for use somewhere in your setting?

    If yes, what year was this computer purchased?

- What is your budget?
- What do you see the webcam being used for most?
- Do you prefer to record video in high definition (HD)?
- How often do you anticipate using the camera?

Using Videoconferencing and Webcams to Support Learning

Teachers can use videoconferencing and webcams to enhance classroom experiences in several ways. Webcams open up countless doors to the classroom as they invite individuals and experts from all over into the classroom. They expand the community of the classroom beyond the physical walls, as illustrated in the experience Rachel and Jennifer provided for their class.

Specific strategies for using videoconferencing and webcams to support learning include

- ✓ support self-confidence and literacy skills,
- ✓ build school community and global awareness,
- ✓ connect with authors,
- ✓ invite experts into the classroom, and
- ✓ encourage family involvement.

SUPPORT SELF-CONFIDENCE AND LITERACY SKILLS

First-grade teacher Cora Boucher wants her students to feel proud and confident in their reading abilities. As she observed the attitudes of her students while they read, she noticed that some readers lacked a confidence she felt they needed to continue on their journey as developing readers. Cora wanted to find an experience that would empower them as readers among peers. She wondered if introducing her students to reading buddies in another city or state would foster the development of confidence and social skills. In her search, she discovered ePals (www.epals.com), a website dedicated to safely connecting classrooms and teachers around the world through digital pen-pal relationships, blogging, project development, special initiatives, and videoconferencing. Through this website and communicating with other colleagues, Cora identified a fifth-grade class that she began collaborating with. Cora and the fifth-grade teacher paired their students and virtually introduced each child to his reading buddy. After some time spent figuring out scheduling, Cora found a comfortable place when each day a few of the first graders could meet one-on-one with their fifth-grade buddy via webcam. Over time, Cora noticed her students' eagerness to meet and read to their buddies increased. Most important, the students' overall confidence in their reading abilities, outside of their buddy relationships, increased.

BUILD SCHOOL COMMUNITY AND GLOBAL AWARENESS

While collaborating with the distant fifth-grade classroom, Cora's class also developed a special relationship with a fifth-grade class in their own school. A student in fifth grade at Cora's school left to study abroad, and while she was gone, both the first- and fifth-grade classrooms virtually followed her on her many adventures. This fifth grader created a blog that the first and fifth graders were able to read and enjoy together. During the day, the first graders left their classroom and signed into Skype, so when their classmate came online, they could call in the fifth-grade class to have a quick chat and update straight from her location. In this experience, a student across the globe was part of two classrooms—as a learner and a teacher. Skype is a popular instant-messaging program that has a video-chat feature. Two computers, each with a webcam, can connect to each other, and their users can see each other through their computers. This is essentially how individuals can have a virtual face-to-face conversation.

Kindergarten classroom shares stories through a video conference. (*www .redleafpress.org/tech/5-2.aspx*)

CONNECT WITH AUTHORS

Author and illustrator studies are common core-curriculum components used to develop positive attitudes around reading and writing in early childhood classrooms. To develop interest and excitement during these investigations, teachers often choose authors that children are familiar with. Considering the popularity of the authors typically chosen, it can be difficult to bring these authors into classrooms to support the learning process. The Skype an Author Network (http://skypeanauthor.wetpaint.com) provides a valuable resource for teachers and librarians to help children connect with authors. This website offers a community of authors that provides schools with opportunities to engage in communication through videoconferencing. The site is extremely user friendly; teachers can search for authors by name or genre. Popular authors such as Todd Parr and Jean Marzollo are part of this community. When authors are not able to physically visit the classroom, the Skype an Author Network provides an opportunity for authors to virtually visit a classroom or library, where students can ask questions, make comments, or hear the authors read their books. This experience helps young children connect to authors and begin to identify themselves as authors. A kindergarten class using Skype to talk with Todd Parr may ask him about how he creates his artwork or why he sometimes chooses to use animals in his books instead of people. A class using Skype to talk with Jean Marzollo may ask her what her favorite children's book is or what it is like to work with Walter Wick on their popular *I Spy* book series. Children in preschool can participate in videoconference conversations in various ways as well. Preschool teachers should provide significant preparation for such an experience and more of a structure during these conversations. They may develop questions ahead of time and send them to the author to review before the conversation. Children in the primary grades have the ability to develop questions in the moment, so less structure is needed in these conversations. These experiences are extremely meaningful and authentic to children when done in a way that is respectful of their knowledge and development.

INVITE EXPERTS INTO THE CLASSROOM

Many young children invest much of their imagination in characters who provide them power, such as kings, queens, princesses, and superheroes. In a class where this interest is particularly evident, you can harness children's interest and imagination by guiding the children on an investigation of castles. Perhaps the investigation might explore the roles and responsibilities of individuals who live in and around castles. During such an investigation, a virtual visit from an expert on ancient and modern castles might help children explore new concepts. Inviting the virtual visitor to join the class at the beginning of the investigation may be helpful in sparking high interest and the development of inquiry questions. Alternatively or additionally, depending on the availability of the guest, consider inviting the virtual visitor to join toward the end of the investigation. This allows time for children to seek answers to individual inquiry questions.

Another way to include experts is by using Google+, a social media site that provides an opportunity to bring people together via video. In the classroom, multiple experts can be invited together to share knowledge with the students. In doing so, individuals from multiple locations can come together in a single video chat room and communicate. This experience can enhance the research process, particularly for children in second and third grade and older, because they are able to collect various perspectives on theories and ideas from knowledgeable individuals.

With the use of webcams, teachers can use children's natural interest as an entry point into an investigation that may not otherwise appear interesting if presented in a different format. Welcoming virtual visitors into your classroom can help children authentically access information that may otherwise be difficult to access.

ENCOURAGE FAMILY INVOLVEMENT

In early childhood classrooms, teachers provide opportunities for their students to realize that every individual, including themselves, is in some way a reader. Some teachers invite children to bring in favorite books from home to share with the class. Some teachers take moments to share favorites of their own. As a child, I enjoyed reading *The Tub People* by Pam Conrad (1989) over and over again. Recently, as my mother went through boxes at her house, she found the book I had loved as a child. When she passed the book on to me, I had to share it with my preschool class. When I brought the book in, I held it on my lap and described how my mom had found a treasure over the weekend, a treasure I had forgotten about. I shared the book with the class and placed it in our reading corner.

In addition to educators sharing books, parents or other important people in the families of the children in a class can bring their favorite books in to share. To build excitement about these classroom guests, consider implementing a weekly secret reader. Readers bring in a book meaningful to them and share a story behind it. After reading the book, it can be left in the classroom for the children to enjoy. But the truth is that families' schedules can be busy, and taking the time to come and visit the classroom during the day can be difficult or impossible. Providing opportunities for family members to use

Family members are knowledgeable individuals and can participate in supporting children's literacy development and love for reading. When family members model reading as teachers do, they show they are readers. As adults and other children read around them in various contexts, young children soon learn that they are not readers just at school; they can be readers anywhere and everywhere.

videoconferencing programs can widen the possibilities of who can share with the class. Videoconferencing also provides family members who live in a different area an opportunity to share a book with the class. In moments like these, using a projector can create the experience and help make it feel as though the reader is right in the room with the children. Details on how to use projectors in the classroom are described in chapter 3.

Using Videoconferencing and Webcams to Support Assessment

Videoconferencing experiences using webcams can provide teachers with opportunities to gather information on children's growth and development. They can also be used to gather information on their own instructional decisions. Because webcams provide the opportunity to record and play back experiences, they offer opportunities for teachers to collaborate and reflect with other teachers and administrators on the assessment data they collect. Teachers can use videoconferencing and webcams to assess

- ✓ comprehension and knowledge of books through book reviews,
- ✓ effectiveness of room arrangement, and
- ✓ administrative support.

COMPREHENSION AND KNOWLEDGE OF BOOKS THROUGH BOOK REVIEWS

As children learn and develop their own criteria for what makes a book interesting to them, they begin to develop an understanding that each reader likes and dislikes certain books. In order to foster further development of this understanding, a kindergarten or early elementary teacher can play short video book reviews given by children in older grades. When children in first grade watch a video book review given by a second or third grader, they can see that children just a few years older have developed the ability to read a book, discuss its contents, and then share it with others. After viewing these videos and discussing the elements of a book review, the first-grade teacher can invite the children to select books they are familiar with to try doing their own book reviews in pairs. After giving their reviews in pairs, the children can provide feedback for one another, discussing any missing pieces. You can set up a book-review recording studio equipped with a desktop or laptop computer and a webcam. The children can visit the book-review recording studio to record their book reviews. Then, to celebrate their recordings, the book reviews can be projected onto a screen to be viewed by the class. Book reviews can also be shared with families and friends outside the school by posting them to a classroom web page.

In order to reflect on each child's book review, teachers can use the Book Review Reflection Guide (form 5.1) to determine which elements were present or missing in the review. Gathering information unique to each child allows you to develop individualized goals and experiences needed to support the children you teach.

EFFECTIVENESS OF ROOM ARRANGEMENT

As you set up your classroom, it is important to reflect on how the children move through the space. After observing the children in the space for a day or sometimes a week, make any necessary changes so children can access materials and spaces independently. As the year moves on, it is still important to

5.1 Book Review Reflection Guide

Name: Charlotte		Book Title: That's Me, Tyler!		
Grade: 3		Author: Frances Burton		
Date: 3/24/11		Illustrator: Karmen Thompson		
Elements of Book Review:		Yes	No	N/A
Title		X		
Author/Illustrator		X		
Topic/Plot		X		
Setting		X		
Characters		X		
Problem/Issue		X		
Acknowledgment of similar books and/or authors			X	
Indications of what student liked about this book		X		

Notes for Future Learning Experiences

In our next reading conference, anchor our conversation in thinking about other books that Charlotte thinks of when reading her current book, *The Tales of Despereaux* by Kate DiCamillo

5.2 Movement Observation Reflection Sheet

WEBCAM REVIEW

Learning Experience: Self-selected centers			Date: 5/9/11	
Observations:			Yes	No
Children are able to access materials in centers provided.				X
Children are able to comfortably sit in their designated areas.			X	
Enough materials are available at each center.			X	
Large furniture is not in the way of pathways.			X	
Individuals with a wheelchair can access all areas in room.			X	
Children do not have access to cords or harmful electrical devices.			X	
Children have enough space to house all personal belongings.			X	
Children ask one another for help when necessary.			X	
Walls are clear of peeling paint.			X	
Chairs in various sizes are available to children.			X	

To-Do List	Plan to Complete
Continue observing children's access to materials. Consider talking to other teachers about their learning center organizers.	Visit first-grade classroom next week to see how the materials in their centers are organized. Hold a class meeting next week to talk with the class about their access to the materials in the centers.

maintain an awareness of how children are moving throughout the classroom. A one-time revision is not enough. When video cameras are not available, webcams can help capture the ways children move throughout the room. Choose a point in the day when a computer equipped with a camera is not being used, and have the camera pointed so it can capture as much classroom activity as possible. After turning the camera on to record, you can go about your normal day with the children, whether that is working in small groups or working one-on-one. Later, you can review the footage to see how children moved throughout the classroom, observing for successful independence or spaces that need revisions. The Movement Observation Reflection Sheet (form 5.2) can help focus your viewing of the video, helping to identify instances that may easily go unnoticed.

ADMINISTRATIVE SUPPORT

Today, principals and other administrative leaders are under pressures that do not always permit them to support classroom teachers as much as they might prefer. When an administrator is in classrooms, young children can feel intimidated if they are not familiar with her. Administrators also want to cause the least amount of intrusion when observing in classrooms in order to gather as much—and as accurate—information about the children's skills and the teacher's practices as possible. In order for administrators to support teachers in such a way, they might consider using a webcam to observe particular classroom experiences. For example, if a teacher is looking for support on how to carry out a classroom meeting, an administrator might observe the meeting using a webcam rather than observing directly. Observing through a webcam would preserve the high level of conversation among the children and reduce any possibilities of children feeling reluctant to share because of the presence of an unfamiliar individual. Later, the teacher and administrator could reflect on the meeting and discuss procedures and skill sets of individual children.

Using Videoconferencing and Webcams to Exhibit Learning

Webcams can be used to share classroom learning. Teachers can share what a child has learned with parents during parent-teacher conferences, and children can share what they have learned with other children and long-distance family members. When parents feel knowledgeable about their child's progress and learning, they can better contribute to their child's continuing growth and development. As children share their knowledge with others using webcams, they see the value in sharing and celebrating knowledge. Videoconferencing and webcams can be used to exhibit learning in the following ways:

- ✓ host parent-teacher conferences,
- ✓ talk with cross-country classrooms, and
- ✓ connect with long-distance relatives.

HOST PARENT-TEACHER CONFERENCES

In the business world, people hold videoconferences when team members or clients are in varying locations and schedules do not allow for everyone to meet in person. The situation can be the same for teachers and families. While phone conferences with family members who cannot attend in person are still a valid option, videoconferencing programs allow you to see the person you're talking with and show work samples as part of the live conversation. This way, family members learn valuable information about their child's growth and development.

Teachers and families who choose to use videoconferencing programs to conduct their conferences can take advantage of a variety of options. In the conference, teachers can speak about particular work samples, and they can refer to them visually, pointing out particular items to highlight. Some programs, such as Skype and iChat, allow the main user to screen-share with the viewers. In this case, you can open up a child's e-portfolio on the screen of the parent's computer. While viewing the e-portfolio, parents can view scanned work samples, photographs, and videos. With the possibilities in videoconferencing programs, teachers have the ability to make the long-distance parent-teacher conference experience almost as real as meeting in person.

TALK WITH CROSS-COUNTRY CLASSROOMS

You can also use videoconferencing programs to share student learning with a class in another town, state, or country. After finding a classroom partner, work with the other teacher to identify a common area of study, such as exploring and learning about community neighborhoods. Then both classes can conduct their investigation with the idea that in the end they will present new learning to the other classroom. As the children learn about their neighborhood and community through taking walks, conducting interviews, reviewing photographs and videos, drawing pictures, and reading books, they can begin to collect items or artifacts to help articulate their learning later to the other class. The classes might consider taking a video of their walks or interviews. They might create a computer file housing some photographs that were particularly interesting or educating in their journey. As their presentation date nears, help your students electronically organize the videos and photographs they wish to share. While sharing their learning with the other class, you can utilize the screen-sharing technique described in the parent-teacher conference example to show photographs collected or videos taken. Switching back to the webcam, small groups of children can share the questions they had, the answers they found, and what resources they used to find their answers. This entire process provides children with an authentic audience with whom to share their learning. In taking the role of the audience, children learn and develop knowledge and respect for other regions. While the children share their learning, they are required to reflect and articulate their learning process, which is a demanding but necessary metacognitive skill.

CONNECT WITH LONG-DISTANCE RELATIVES

It is not uncommon for children to have family members living in another city, state, or country. Webcams can be used to videoconference with these relatives, providing children with the opportunity to share their work and learning. Schools often have a "Grandparents Day" or "Grandfriends Day," on which these important individuals are invited to come and visit classrooms. When children have grandparents or grandfriends in distant places, teachers can use webcams to provide an opportunity for these individuals to visit the classroom for a virtual tour and see the work of children as they hold it up in front of the camera. Webcams can truly expand the walls of classrooms.

◆   ◆   ◆

When children are given opportunities to speak, ask questions, and make observations, they are able to process and apply information. Webcams and videoconferencing experiences provide children with valuable opportunities to engage in conversation with those outside of the physical classroom. This technology allows the classroom walls to come down and include individuals on the other side of the globe. These experiences allow children to reflect on situations, problem solve, and plan for the future. Young children need concrete opportunities to explore concepts. Webcams provide a developmentally appropriate way to engage with concepts that could otherwise be abstract.

» TOOLBOX TIPS

CHOOSING A VIDEOCONFERENCING PROGRAM

Beginning the process of identifying a videoconferencing program can be daunting. There are a variety of them out there; however, many of them are intended for the business world, where larger, more frequent conferences are held. Below is a list of common and virtually free programs. Most of these programs can be used on either PC or Apple computers. When determining videoconferencing programs, it is important to consider these questions:

- What type of computer do you have (PC or Apple)?
- What do you intend to use the videoconferencing program for?
- Will you at some time want to videoconference with more than one other person/location?
- Do you want file-sharing options?
- Do you want instant-messaging options?

These questions will help you in your exploration of the various video-conferencing programs available. Below are a few of the popular programs used today. Other programs are available that may meet your specific needs or restrictions.

PROGRAM	COST	PC/APPLE
Skype	Free	Both
ePals	Free	Both
ooVoo	Free	Both
iChat	Free	Apple
AIM	Free	Both
Gmail Chat	Free	Both
Google+	Free	Both
FaceTime	Free	Apple

Forms

⑤

5.1 Book Review Reflection Guide

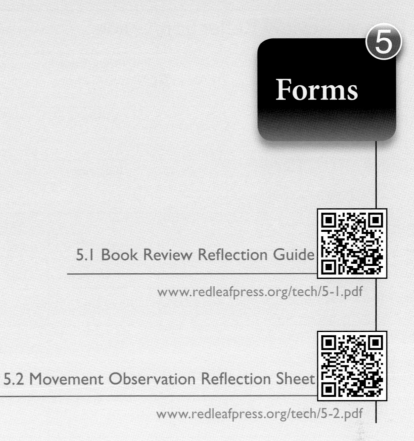

www.redleafpress.org/tech/5-1.pdf

5.2 Movement Observation Reflection Sheet

www.redleafpress.org/tech/5-2.pdf

5.1 Book Review Reflection Guide

Name:	Book Title:
Grade:	Author:
Date:	Illustrator:

Elements of Book Review:	Yes	No	N/A
Title			
Author/Illustrator			
Topic/Plot			
Setting			
Characters			
Problem/Issue			
Acknowledgment of similar books and/or authors			
Indications of what student liked about this book			

Notes for Future Learning Experiences

5.2 Movement Observation Reflection Sheet

WEBCAM REVIEW

Learning Experience:		Date:	
Observations:		Yes	No
Children are able to access materials in centers provided.			
Children are able to comfortably sit in their designated areas.			
Enough materials are available at each center.			
Large furniture is not in the way of pathways.			
Individuals with a wheelchair can access all areas in room.			
Children do not have access to cords or harmful electrical devices.			
Children have enough space to house all personal belongings.			
Children ask one another for help when necessary.			
Walls are clear of peeling paint.			
Chairs in various sizes are available to children.			

To-Do List	Plan to Complete

6
Sharing Knowledge and Learning through Publication and Presentation Tools

www.redleafpress.org/tech/6-1.aspx

Kindergarten teachers Barb Fisher and Lauren Cohen know it is important to open their school year with content that acknowledges the many anxieties children experience during their transition to full-day school. In order to help their students, they open their school year with exploring feelings. This provides their students the opportunity to discuss what makes them feel excited, scared, eager, nervous, and so on. Barb and Lauren look for ways to integrate multiple important concepts in their units. They know that young children oftentimes experience frustration as they begin to learn to write. In order to help the children develop the idea that they are authors, they decided to help their classes create a feelings book. They are aware of the new ways people gather and enjoy literature, so rather than creating a paper book, they helped their classes create an e-book. First, they discussed an author's process of creating both paper and e-books. Then photographs were taken of the children depicting particular feelings. The children's voices describing the photographs were recorded and included in the e-book.

They also discussed the ways the author works with all sorts of people to celebrate the book's publication. In their classrooms, they planned a release party. In this party, the children were able to enjoy snacks, share their favorite parts of the process, and of course view their e-book on a large screen. During the celebration, one of the classroom assistants heard one of the children say, "This is the best day ever!"

Embedded in the publication processes, children learn the importance of style and creativity, and they learn reasons for particular sequences. Children can learn that an author's books have a certain style; for example, words on a page may rhyme. Similarly, they can learn how an illustrator might use different mediums to illustrate a particular feeling. Soon children learn how these elements relate directly to their own development of style and creativity. As children embark on these journeys of development and exploration, they see the value of hard work and effort.

Strategies that involve children publishing and presenting content and new knowledge require a greater amount of support. This support can be introduced to students by explaining how material published and presented in the "real world" requires many individuals to work together. This is true for the classroom as well; the support just looks different.

As young children develop a sense of agency, they begin to take great pride in their work and effort. Evidence of this is visible when a toddler shouts, "Look, Mom, look—I put on my own shirt!" This pride commonly carries on into the preschool and school years. There have been countless times when I have had children enter my classroom in the morning with loud, confident announcements, such as "Mr. Puerling, I hopped three whole times on the way to school this morning and didn't fall down!" or "Today I chose a Nutella sandwich for lunch at school, and I've never tried it before. We will see what happens at lunch today!" Considering this developmental marker, teachers can use this pride as a vehicle for children to learn and explore important skills and concepts. As introduced in chapter 4, when teachers help children find ways to celebrate their work and effort through various ways of publishing, children develop increased self-confidence and a willingness to try new things. Creating and assembling materials into a state ready for publication or presentation takes more than one person, no matter what the project may be. An editor helps an author identify the best way to present content. A graphic designer works with a marketing specialist to create a logo for a company. Collaboration happens on many levels during our daily lives. Considering the collaborative nature of publication and presentation, many of the strategies provided in this chapter include levels of collaboration with others.

Using Publication and Presentation Tools to Support Learning

The process of publishing any information is complex and layered; it is collaborative and reflective. Teachers can help children understand various forms of publication and the steps within them by giving children an opportunity to actually publish their own information. Within these opportunities, children will learn to respect the work of authors, illustrators, singers, artists, and researchers. When children have the opportunity to try on the roles and responsibilities of these jobs, they develop an understanding of their own work and intentions. Teachers can provide experiences in which children use publication and presentation tools to

✓ develop classroom newsletters,

✓ create invitations for classroom and school events,

✓ write informational articles,

✓ publish nonfiction books,

✓ make books inspired by familiar authors, and

✓ produce video books.

DEVELOP CLASSROOM NEWSLETTERS

For years, teachers have sent home newsletters to families reminding them about permission slips due, upcoming school or classroom events, and perhaps items on the classroom wish list. With the technology at your fingertips and the skills that children are learning early on, you can rethink how you develop newsletters. Invite children into the creation and publication of a classroom newsletter. In getting this started, familiarize children with the purposes and features of newsletters by showing them previous classroom or school newsletters. After children have a firm understanding of what a newsletter is intended to do and how writers collect information, establish teams of writers in which children divide up roles and responsibilities to complete their own newsletter. A team model approach encourages children to work together to negotiate roles and decisions (Wang et al. 2010). Consider creating job or position titles for the roles and responsibilities of those involved in creating the newsletter. In elementary school classrooms, teams of three or four news reporters can work together to determine classroom experiences and events to highlight. They can also work together to conduct interviews or surveys of students, parents, and teachers. Or they can describe a learning experience illustrated in a drawing or exhibited in a photograph they took. Once the teams have conducted any necessary interviews, created any artwork, or taken any necessary photographs, they need to finalize their text. Then you can help the class upload and assemble the materials into a newsletter template provided by Microsoft Word or Pages.

While assembling the newsletter, the teams can personalize it by choosing particular fonts to convey a mood or effect. Once complete, help the class to print a copy of the newsletter for review. After reviewing it and making any necessary changes, they can visit the printing press, also known as the staff copy machine, to create the necessary number of copies to be distributed to each student and shared with others. If the newsletter can also be published electronically, the teams can post it to the class website or send it out via e-mail to their families.

Including the teams in the entire process, from making the initial decisions to passing out the final newsletter, helps them see how their work and effort can come full circle. Providing them with the opportunity to work with Microsoft Word or Pages builds in authentic moments to learn how to use a program. Having the students work together in small groups offers them an opportunity to develop necessary social skills and to learn the value of collaboration. Printing out a draft of the newsletter for their review offers them an opportunity to evaluate their work and make changes to enhance or make it more articulate. Bringing them to the copy machine allows them to see their work being duplicated and to get a taste of how newspapers are made. Giving them the opportunity to share and distribute the newsletter to their peers requires them to describe their process and defend why they chose particular events to highlight. Providing an e-publishing option helps the children begin to understand the multitude of ways to share information, while at the same time modeling an authentic and meaningful use of the Internet and e-mail.

CREATE INVITATIONS FOR CLASSROOM AND SCHOOL EVENTS

When particularly important classroom events are planned, invite small groups of children to help with each particular part of the planning, including creating invitations. You can invite a few children to be a team of assistant classroom-event coordinators. They can work together to create an invitation for the event. In this experience, the team would develop a design to convey important information, such as place, time, date, what to bring, whom to contact if one is going to come, and who to contact if one has questions. This experience invites particularly interested children to take part in the planning of meaningful events in their classroom. Like the news reporter team, this team works together on a novel project, developing unique collaborative skills necessary for later life experiences.

It is important to be thoughtful in how you structure the groups for these experiences. Working in groups of individuals is difficult even for adults. Be sure that the choices you make for these groups set them up for success. You may want to consider personalities and strengths when matching children up.

WRITE INFORMATIONAL ARTICLES

A teacher in a second- or third-grade classroom, teaching the basics of informational articles, might have the students work in small teams of journalists to create informational articles on a particular animal or a specific interest within a content-area investigation. After looking at articles in *Time for Kids* or *National Geographic Kids*, children can begin to learn how nonfiction articles often include features such as charts, graphs, and captions. As they learn these features, they also begin to learn the difference between a story and an article. After a substantial number of experiences with various articles and periodicals written for children, they can take on the role of a journalist to write their own articles. In their teams, they can identify what exactly from their research they wish to include in their article. After you review the information and photographs they wish to include, the teams can work with you or a volunteer to upload and assemble their articles. After completing the articles, an article anthology can be created for the classroom library. Placing the anthology in the classroom library conveys the idea that their efforts and ideas are just as valuable as those put into the other published texts present in the library. To share their learning outside the classroom, copies of the articles can be sent home with families or posted to a classroom website.

PUBLISH NONFICTION BOOKS

Publishing a book is a lengthy process that takes an amazing amount of thinking, collaboration, and decision making. Children are typically completely unaware of the process necessary for a book to appear in their hands. Providing children with opportunities to publish their writing for others is a powerful way to help children appreciate all books—and learn a lot about the publication process. Publishing in collaborative groups improves critical-thinking and problem-solving skills (Greaves et al. 2010). And it helps children see school as a meaningful place to learn and interact with the world. You can help children develop their writing skills, understand the process of writing a book, experience collaboration, and value the knowledge of others when they work collaboratively and creatively. Shutterfly and Snapfish are web-based photo-processing centers where users can upload, share, copy, retouch, print, and order photographs. It's possible to create a variety of projects: from placing a photo on a mug to creating a personalized book filled with photographs and anecdotes describing them. Publish photo books to help children explore the publication and collaborative processes. When I taught preschool, as I mentioned in chapter 2, the children investigated Australian animals. To learn about these unique creatures, children interacted with puppets, photographs, artifacts, popular Australian artwork,

No matter what age level you work with, children are developing social-emotional skills. Ben Kovacs and I decided to work together to address a number of goals we had for the children. One common goal was for each child to learn how to work with someone who was not the same age, had different interests, and had a different skill set for gathering information.

picture books, and informational books. Through the investigation, the children's interest and motivation to learn more about the animals increased. In this investigation, I partnered with sixth-grade teacher Ben Kovacs.

We paired our classes up into small groups of learning partners so that the collaborative work they were about to embark on would be most meaningful. Ben and I decided to invite the learning partners to work together to write a nonfiction book on Australian animals. Each preschool child chose an animal she wanted to know more about and developed a question about that animal. While the preschoolers were busy learning about the various Australian animals and developing their questions, their sixth-grade learning partners were learning about effective research strategies and appropriate research resources. The preschoolers' questions were given to the sixth graders, who then had to use their new research skills to find answers to later share with their preschool partners.

After the preschoolers learned answers from their learning partners, together they created a sentence statement that answered the question. Together, the learning partners illustrated a page with their sentence using the Australian aboriginal style of dot art. Ben and I then scanned the pages into Shutterfly and published the book using its Custom Path photo book program. Both the preschool and sixth-grade classroom purchased numerous copies of the book for the classroom library. In this experience, the preschool children explored a whole host of social and academic skills. They learned that they could work and collaborate with children older

than themselves. Moreover, they learned that they did not need to be afraid of older children. The preschoolers learned that their questions and answers were something to be shared with others. They developed an awareness of a variety of Australian animals. Finally, they felt the pride and celebration that published authors feel when they hold their own bound book in their hands.

During this investigation, Ben's class was learning about reliable research resources. With their participation in this partnership, the sixth graders were given an authentic opportunity to use some of the resources and strategies they had been learning. The sixth graders also learned about the cognitive capacities of younger children, and they learned how to speak to young children in ways preschoolers could understand. They also learned strategies for keeping young children engaged. After a joint field trip to a zoo, one of the sixth graders told Ben, "Now I know how my parents feel!"

MAKE BOOKS INSPIRED BY FAMILIAR AUTHORS

Classrooms can also use Shutterfly or Snapfish to publish books as a class rather than in a learning partner structure. Kira Hamann took her preschool class on a journey of publication in the midst of their author study of Mo Willems. When Kira noticed her preschoolers' love for his books increase over a short period of time, she offered them an opportunity to write their own book using Willems's style. They were ecstatic and began their adventure immediately. They voted on which familiar style they would use and chose his pigeon book style. Next, they broke into collaborative groups where, with the help of another teacher or classroom assistant, group members decided on the characters, plot, medium for illustration, and paper to be used. After these important decisions were made, the children created illustrations to match the plot they had determined. Once the pages were created, Kira scanned the pages into Shutterfly and ordered a book for their classroom. Upon the book's arrival, they held a celebration for the publication of their effort and learning.

Similarly, when I was teaching preschool and carrying out an exciting author study of Laura Numeroff, the children expressed an interest in creating a book like Numeroff's. The class decided they wanted to make a book with a style similar to that of *If You Give Mouse a Cookie*. Each child provided an event for the story and an illustration to match. I then scanned the pages into Shutterfly and awaited the arrival of the book. While waiting, in order to learn more about the publication process, I invited children's author Carol Boas to visit to share her book and story of publication. After reading her book *A Room of My Own*, Carol spoke about how publishers develop a plan for how books will look. After our conversation with her, we watched a video of a book being bound in a binding factory. Just after that, I projected the Shutterfly website onto a large screen, where we were able to see a preview of what our book would look like once it arrived in the mail.

Having a solid understanding of the publication process, the children were overjoyed once the book arrived. After enjoying the book, we discussed how we could celebrate our publication by taking a look at what authors do once they have published a book. After discussing that authors sometimes have book signings to celebrate their books, they unanimously decided they wanted to move forward and plan a book signing. To determine what our book signing event would look like, I projected photographs of actual book signings. After reviewing these photographs, we worked together to create a list of the items necessary for our event: copies of the book, authors, a line of people, pens, and food. After sending home invitations to families, the class posted the book on our classroom website for families to order their own copy. Before the event, we reviewed autographs signed by authors we know. The children learned that Mo Willems writes his name, Carol Boas writes a message and her name, and Todd Parr draws a picture. This was particularly important for young children who were not yet writing. Reviewing the various ways to leave an autograph made each child feel comfortable knowing that wherever they were in their development, their autograph was authentic and similar to those of authors they knew and loved. Once the event came, there were copies of the book, a line of excited family members awaiting their autographs, an assortment of food, and a table lined with assigned seats for the young authors. At each seat, name tents were provided so children could celebrate their participation, help family members unfamiliar with all of the children's names, and provide support to children who wanted to try to write their name as an autograph. When young children know the publication process and see themselves as a learning author and illustrator, skills such as spelling, handwriting, forming sentences, and using correct punctuation have more meaning and can be less intimidating.

As individuals in teacher-preparation programs in colleges and universities learn methods and strategies to support early learning, it is imperative that they learn how technology can be threaded within learning experiences. National Louis University student teacher Alyssa Reihle developed a learning experience to support preschool children in an author study of Walter Wick and Jean Marzollo. Alyssa held a conversation with the class that addressed previously viewed videos of Walter Wick, exploring his process for taking photographs, and learning how Jean Marzollo develops her sentences for each of the photographs. Alyssa invited the children to try this out for themselves by creating their own book styled after Wick and Marzollo's *I Spy* books. Alyssa provided a variety of familiar materials found in the *I Spy* and *Can You See What I See?* books. In small groups, she invited the children to arrange any collection of items to be photographed for their page of the book. Then she gave them the opportunity to take a photo of their collection. Alyssa recognized the range of developmental levels present in the classroom and provided support for each child when she noticed it necessary. For example, most of the four- and five-year-old children were able to take their photographs independently, whereas most of the three-year-old children needed assistance. As each group took their photos, Alyssa invited them to review the photograph to determine whether it looked the way they wanted it to. Once the children were satisfied with their photograph, she asked them what they would like readers to find on their page when reading the published book. Alyssa recorded their lists and used them as the text for the pages. Next she developed the photographs, fastened them to sheets of paper, and bound the pages. She brought the book in and shared it with the class. Once she had shared the book, she placed the book, like all other publications, in the classroom library to be enjoyed anytime.

Kindergarten and first grade students work on publishing their own e-books. (*www.redleafpress.org/tech/6-2.aspx*)

PRODUCE VIDEO BOOKS

At Butler Elementary School in the Springfield School District in Illinois, David Curry is a K–2 teacher for children with special needs. David's goal for some of his students is for them to be able to write five complete sentences related to a specific topic. To support these children in developing this skill, David invites them to create video books. He sees this strategy as a highly motivational, exciting, and meaningful way for children to explore developing literacy skills. To begin the process, David has the children write sentences at their instructional reading and writing level. After making sure these sentences maintain a focus on the chosen topic, he invites the children to create illustrations that match their sentences. Having created the sentences and illustrations, David helps the children record an audio reading of their work using QuickTime on his Apple computer. The audio file is imported to iTunes. Then David works with the children to capture digital images of the sentences and illustrations, using a digital camera or iPod camera feature, and these images are saved to Apple's iMovie program.

David then works within iMovie to combine the audio recording and digital images to publish the video books. Video books made by David's students can be found on his web page: www.springfield.k12.il.us/teachers /dlcurry/?p=1525&b=4. David has observed that the students who have created video books become more excited about writing and publishing books. He has also noticed that the excitement and pride results in the students' increased willingness to try new things within their literacy development.

In making the video books, David's classroom utilizes Apple computers and programs. Video books can also be made on PC computers using programs such as Windows Movie Maker, Windows Live Movie Maker, and Corel Digital Studio. Ways to publish and create video books using iPad applications are explored in chapter 8.

Using Publication and Presentation Tools to Support Assessment

Published and presented work and material provides teachers with an opportunity to gather a wealth of valuable information on children's growth and development. When children share their published work, they should be asked to describe their process, plan, and intention. Classmates should be encouraged to ask questions so each child can elaborate on elements through discussion. While children discuss these elements, teachers learn about the children and therefore learn how to support them in future experiences.

Teachers can use publication and presentation tools to assess

✓ participation in newsletter creation and publication team,

✓ ongoing contributions in collaborative experiences, and

✓ progress toward goals in published video books.

PARTICIPATION IN NEWSLETTER CREATION AND PUBLICATION TEAM

As described earlier in the chapter, children can cocreate a classroom newsletter to announce and celebrate learning experiences, events, artwork, and books the class is currently reading and enjoying. During and after this experience, teachers can assess how the students are able to take on the roles of researcher, writer, and reporter. They can also look at how each child works with his or her team to ask questions, generate ideas, collect materials, and write or draw

6.1 Newsletter Participation Reflection Sheet

Child: **Mara** Date: **2/18/11**

Other Group Members:
Ursula, Henry, and David

Child contributed to group conversations by:

Asking questions	Yes X	No
Answering questions	Yes X	No
Making suggestions	Yes X	No
Compromising	Yes X	No

Child utilized classroom resources to develop ideas:

Photographs	Yes X	No	N/A
Printed books, audiobooks, e-books, digital books	Yes X	No	N/A
Videos	Yes X	No	N/A
Other children	Yes X	No	N/A
Teachers/adults	Yes X	No	N/A

Child was able to:

Carry out tasks determined by group	Yes X	No
Utilize writing and drawing skills to convey ideas	Yes X	No

Notes for future learning experiences:
In the past, Mara has appeared timid while talking with other staff and faculty members. Next week, send her on an errand to her first-grade teacher Ms Caro. After her errand, talk to her about what made it easy to talk to Ms. Caro. Use this conversation as a bridge into a conversation about what makes her uncomfortable talking to other teachers in the building.

6.2 Newsletter Participation Self-Reflection Sheet

News Reporter: **Mara** Date: **2/18/11**

Describe how you helped your group with the newsletter:

I thought I was helpful when the group needed someone to get a photograph from the top of the playground. I felt brave enough to climb up and take the photograph.

I also thought I was helpful when the our group needed some resources on playgrounds. I went on the Internet at home with my parents, and we printed out some website pages to help us learn more about the different types of playgrounds.

Teacher notes for future learning experiences:

In our next class meeting, talk about how we can use the Internet with parents to conduct research at home!

necessary items. The Newsletter Participation Reflection Sheet (form 6.1) is available to organize this assessment. Using this reflection sheet provides valuable information about how children work in small groups on a specific task and how they are able to take responsibility to complete the task. The reflection sheet also helps track the degree to which individual children can write about a topic. As part of the assessment process, it is important to know how the children feel about their participation in the process. The Newsletter Participation Self-Reflection Sheet (form 6.2) provides an opportunity to help children understand that they can be part of their own assessment. This self-assessment tool helps children reflect on their participation and organize their thoughts on the experience. It also helps children practice developing metacognitive skills as they look back on the process as a whole.

Teachers interested in learning more about small-group collaborative work are encouraged to review the book *Comprehension and Collaboration: Inquiry Circles in Action* by Stephanie Harvey and Harvey Daniels (2009). The book includes a companion DVD that shows how a first-grade teacher can carry out inquiry-group investigations.

ONGOING CONTRIBUTIONS IN COLLABORATIVE EXPERIENCES

A variety of literacy skills, content areas, and social skills can be assessed while publishing books. As children meet with their learning partners, teachers can take ongoing anecdotal notes to track children's consistency and progress. Below is an example of a set of skills addressed in the process of collaboratively creating and publishing the book on Australian animals. At the bottom of each column, an assessment is listed. The Literacy Snapshot Assessment (form 6.3), Content Area Snapshot Assessment (form 6.4), or Collaboration Snapshot

LITERACY SKILL/CONCEPT	CONTENT AREA CONCEPT	SOCIAL SKILL/CONCEPT
Difference between a question and a comment	Animals in Australia are different from animals found here in the United States.	People can work together on a single task.
Developing sentences related to each other	Animals in Australia can live in water and on land.	People ask how they can help when working in groups.
Difference in roles between an author and an illustrator	Australian animals can be marsupials.	People are similar and different in many ways.
LITERACY SNAPSHOT (form 6.3)	CONTENT AREA SNAPSHOT (form 6.4)	COLLABORATION SNAPSHOT (form 6.5)

Assessment (form 6.5) can be used to record the progress of individual children. These ongoing assessments can help you determine how children work with other children on various tasks and whether they are understanding and applying a particular skill or concept.

In organizing the skills addressed in collaborative experiences such as the Australian animal book creation, it is important to thoughtfully plan how you will embed assessment of the children's acquisition of skills and concepts. The provided assessments can help you focus the way you gather information about children in ongoing experiences. When these notes are taken over time and reviewed for progress, you can identify particular children who need additional experiences with specific skills. These assessments can also be helpful for teaching partners to use when planning future collaborative learning experiences.

PROGRESS TOWARD GOALS IN PUBLISHED VIDEO BOOKS

When children create and publish video books, teachers can use the Video Book Reflection Sheet (form 6.6) to explore literacy skills evident in a process and the finished product. This assessment can help you determine the progress a child is making toward a particular skill or goal. As you identify progress, you can plan additional experiences to further support children. As teachers develop

6.3 Literacy Snapshot Assessment

Child: Richard		Date: 6/2/11	
Task at hand: Brainstorm how their illustration will look.			
Literacy skill/concept: Difference between a question and a comment			
Actively participating in task at hand		Yes X	No
Appears to understand skill/concept		Yes X	No
Needs additional experiences with skill/concept		Yes	No X

Evidence:
When Richard's learning partner asked him to get a scissors, Richard announced, "Sure I can get a scissors. I will be right back. Is there anything else we need?"

With Richard responding with an answer that addressed the original question, and then extending the conversation with a relevant question of his own, he shows understanding of the difference between a question and a comment.

6.4 Content Area Snapshot Assessment

Child: William		Date: 6/2/11	
Task at hand: Brainstorm how their illustration will look.			
Content area concept: Animals in Australia are different from animals found here in the United States.			
Actively participating in task at hand		Yes X	No
Appears to understand concept		Yes X	No
Needs additional experiences with concept		Yes	No X

Evidence:
When William's partner asked him if would ever want to go to Australia to see where kangaroos live, William responded, "I don't need to. I'm going to go to the zoo; they live there."

In order to help William understand the difference between where kangaroos come from and a zoo where some animals live, I will need to make sure to have a conversation him about this on our field trip to the zoo next week.

6.5 Collaboration Snapshot Assessment

Child: James		Date: 6/2/11	
Task at hand: Brainstorm how their illustration will look.			
Actively participating in task at hand		Yes X	No
Working with learning partner without social conflict		Yes X	No
Appears to feel comfortable		Yes X	No

Evidence:
James appeared to work with his learning partner without any conflicts. They remained on task, finished their task, and enjoyed a book together after finishing.

goals for their students and align experiences to achieve these goals, they are exercising intentional teaching. The Video Book Reflection Sheet can facilitate intentional teaching by helping teachers remain aware of their goals for children and the specific progress children are making toward their goals. These goals, when thoughtfully developed, provide necessary, individualized experiences for each child. When goals are monitored over time, you can be aware of whether the goals are on track or need to be revised to better meet the child where he or she is at developmentally.

6.6 Video Book Reflection Sheet			
Child: Jo-jo		Date: 6/2/11	
Goal: Write a nonfiction book with 3 to 4 important pieces of information the reader could learn.			
Title of video book: My Summer Camp			
Evidence of attempting to achieve goal		Yes X	No
Evidence of achieving goal		Yes X	No
Needs additional experiences to achieve goal		Yes X	No
Plans for future learning experiences Jo-jo was able to write a nonfiction book that told 4 facts about the summer camp he will be participating in over the summer. In a future book, I am going to nudge Jo-jo to try a book with 5–6 facts included throughout.			

Using Publication and Presentation Tools to Exhibit Learning

When authors finally publish a book, they want to share the book with everyone they know, whether this is done by word of mouth, a journal article, an e-mail blast from a publisher, or at a conference. When children embark on their own journeys through the writing process, teachers can help them celebrate their efforts and collaboration in similar ways. As children share their publications with others (peers, teachers, family members, or the greater community), they describe their process and share their journey. They help viewers and readers of their work understand their intention. In doing so, children use these publication and presentation experiences to share their learning. Teachers and children can

✓ share published books with families and

✓ share learning through student-created podcasts.

SHARE PUBLISHED BOOKS WITH FAMILIES

Teachers need to help parents understand their children's social and academic gains. Sharing publications in a parent-teacher conference or other venue offers teachers an opportunity to define and describe the layers of the process. For example, if you are looking at a book with a parent, you can describe how the children first had to decide what they were going to write about and then come up with a plan for what would go on each page. You can describe how the children learn that the publication process takes time—it might take them several days to finish the book. If a parent understands the process a child takes, and what exactly a child learns from that process, the parent can better support and encourage that kind of work at school and at home.

Share video books with families by posting them to your classroom website. Sharing the publication this way not only helps children celebrate their effort; it also helps families with busy schedules keep current on the literacy skills their children are developing. When you post video books, you can also provide a few notes about what a group of children is learning to help families identify and understand some of these specific skills young children develop. For example, consider helping a child develop the ability to create a sequence of logical events. You can describe how the class reviewed some of Laura Numeroff's books, such as *If You Give a Pig a Pancake* or *If You Give a Moose a Muffin,* to see how an author is able to create a series of events that make sense, even when those events are imaginary. You can then present a video book made by the child in which he tried out that skill, using what he learned from Laura Numeroff's books. When teachers provide a context for what is being shared, parents can better understand the relevance and importance of such learning experiences.

Ashley Wales, first-grade teacher, reflects on her class's experience writing and publishing e-books. (*www .redleafpress.org/tech/6-3.aspx*)

SHARE LEARNING THROUGH STUDENT-CREATED PODCASTS

Since children typically enjoy sharing their thoughts and ideas if someone will listen, harness this enjoyment to elicit information about what they are learning. Using Apple programs such as Photo Booth, iMovie, and GarageBand, or PC programs such as Windows Movie Maker or Windows Movie Maker Live, children can record information about particular topics. For example, at the beginning of the year, children learn about the routines of a classroom, such as where the lockers are, where to sit, how to line up, and how to access materials. Many schools hold an event in the first several weeks to which families are invited to come and learn about these routines and other curriculum-related items. To build anticipation for this event and to exhibit how much children learn about routines in the first several weeks of school, a teacher or classroom volunteer can help a small group of children create a podcast to advertise the event. In the podcast, children can discuss some of the things their families will learn by attending the event. This podcast can be posted to a website or e-mailed to families. Similarly, children working on their class newsletter can create a podcast about their experiences as news reporters. They can discuss what it's like to work with other children to make decisions as a group rather than individually and what it was like to watch the copy machine run off the copies of their newsletter to go home that day.

Field trips are powerful experiences for children to connect and apply information to. Teachers and parents can learn about how children connect and apply new information by inviting children to create podcasts about a field trip experience and how it relates to what is being learned in the classroom. Providing families with an opportunity to hear other children reflect on learning experiences can also inform their knowledge of how and what children are learning at these ages.

◆　　　◆　　　◆

Too often the learning that happens in a classroom stays in the classroom. Particularly in early childhood classrooms, too often investigations, new ideas, questions, process, and conclusions are not shared with families, school, and community. When children are given clear purposes for the investigations they embark on and are told the ways in which they and their community will benefit from their learning, they are more likely to invest time and motivation into the process. The experiences become meaningful. It's my hope that the strategies provided in this chapter give you and the children in your classroom developmentally appropriate ways to share their learning.

» TOOLBOX TIPS

PURCHASING PUBLICATION AND PRESENTATION SOFTWARE

The following charts show the features each program includes. Notice that many programs can be used to help carry out a variety of the strategies described in this chapter. Given that teachers utilize PC and/or Apple desktop and laptop computers in schools, the two charts exhibit which programs are needed to carry out strategies depending on the type of computer.

Apple

PROGRAM	ORGANIZE PHOTOS	ORGANIZE VIDEO	ORGANIZE AUDIO	CREATE PODCASTS	CREATE VIDEO BOOKS	CREATE DOCUMENTS
iMovie		X		X	X	
GarageBand			X	X		
iTunes		X	X	X	X	
Pages						X
Keynote				X	X	
iPhoto	X					
RealPlayer		X		X	X	
QuickTime		X		X	X	
PowerPoint				X	X	

PC

PROGRAM	ORGANIZE PHOTOS	ORGANIZE VIDEO	ORGANIZE AUDIO	CREATE PODCASTS	CREATE VIDEO BOOKS	CREATE DOCUMENTS
Microsoft Word						X
Windows Media Player	X	X	X			
Real Player		X	X	X	X	
Windows Live Movie Maker		X	X	X	X	
PowerPoint				X	X	

Forms

6

6.1 Newsletter Participation Reflection Sheet

www.redleafpress.org/tech/6-1.pdf

6.2 Newsletter Participation Self-Reflection Sheet

www.redleafpress.org/tech/6-2.pdf

6.3 Literacy Snapshot Assessment

www.redleafpress.org/tech/6-3.pdf

6.4 Content Area Snapshot Assessment

www.redleafpress.org/tech/6-4.pdf

6.5 Collaboration Snapshot Assessment

www.redleafpress.org/tech/6-5.pdf

6.6 Video Book Reflection Sheet

www.redleafpress.org/tech/6-6.pdf

6.1 Newsletter Participation Reflection Sheet

Child:

Date:

Other Group Members:

Child contributed to group conversations by:

Asking questions	Yes	No
Answering questions	Yes	No
Making suggestions	Yes	No
Compromising	Yes	No

Child utilized classroom resources to develop ideas:

Photographs	Yes	No	N/A
Printed books, audiobooks, e-books, digital books	Yes	No	N/A
Videos	Yes	No	N/A
Other children	Yes	No	N/A
Teachers/adults	Yes	No	N/A

Child was able to:

Carry out tasks determined by group	Yes	No
Utilize writing and drawing skills to convey ideas	Yes	No

Notes for future learning experiences:

6.2 Newsletter Participation Self-Reflection Sheet

News Reporter:	Date:

Describe how you helped your group with the newsletter:

Teacher notes for future learning experiences:

6.3 Literacy Snapshot Assessment

Child:	Date:		
Task at hand:			
Literacy skill/concept:			
Actively participating in task at hand		Yes	No
Appears to understand skill/concept		Yes	No
Needs additional experiences with skill/concept		Yes	No
Evidence:			

6.4 Content Area Snapshot Assessment

Child:	Date:		
Task at hand:			
Content area concept:			
Actively participating in task at hand		Yes	No
Appears to understand concept		Yes	No
Needs additional experiences with concept		Yes	No
Evidence:			

6.5 Collaboration Snapshot Assessment

Child:	Date:

Task at hand:

Actively participating in task at hand	Yes	No
Working with learning partner without social conflict	Yes	No
Appears to feel comfortable	Yes	No

Evidence:

6.6 Video Book Reflection Sheet

Child:	Date:

Goal:

Title of video book:

Evidence of attempting to achieve goal	Yes	No
Evidence of achieving goal	Yes	No
Needs additional experiences to achieve goal	Yes	No

Plans for future learning experiences

7

Using Video Snapshots to Support Inquiry and Expand Classroom Walls

www.redleafpress.org/tech/7-1.aspx

After my wife and I moved into a larger apartment in the city of Chicago, my sister and her husband decided to bring their two children down from northern Wisconsin for a visit. Their son, Jackson, who was three years old at the time of their visit, had been fascinated with trains, and he was looking forward to riding a subway train in Chicago. Long before their visit, my wife and I gave them a copy of *Subway Ride* by Heather Lynn Miller to read with our nephew. *Subway Ride* is full of illustrations from subway trains around the world. Having enjoyed the book several times over the weeks prior to visiting, Jackson fervently asked to see and ride the subway train. Since we couldn't ride the subway train the first day of their visit, I took out my iPad and showed him a few YouTube videos of subway trains in the city of Chicago (not all the trains are elevated). The next day, Jackson was able to ride the Blue Line subway train. While boarding the train, Jackson's dad used his iPhone to record the experience. He captured the roar of the train coming into the station and the mass of people exiting and entering the train. He also captured Jackson's excited yet nervous expression as we all boarded the train. After our day had ended, I sat with Jackson as he operated his father's

iPhone to review the videos taken earlier. At one point, I had the phone in my hand, swiping through the photographs and videos. I touched a photograph, assuming it was a video. At that moment, Jackson took the iPhone from me while announcing, "No, Uncle Brian, you can't play that, that's just a picture." I then watched him swipe to the next available video and play it for me. I was shocked at his ability to recognize the difference between a photograph and a video.

It has been moments like these when I am reminded of the digital age that young children are growing up in. It is amazing that Jackson is able to access so much with his tiny fingers. Having such quick and easy access to videos brings the world closer to us no matter how old we are.

While writing this book, I met David Kleeman. David is a brilliant individual and is the president of the American Center for Children and Media (ACCM). While David and I had lunch on a hot day in early July, I learned what an amazing advocate he is for the development of media programming that supports and encourages early learning. ACCM is dedicated to helping support networks, agencies, and programs in creating children's programming that respects development and well-being. I was so inspired that I asked him to contribute to this book. His words need to be heard. Read below about how David believes that media programming can enhance the lives of children.

Lifelong, we expand our world by building connections upon that which is familiar and demystifying that which is new. Carefully chosen, illustrative images and videos can transform a screen in an early childhood classroom into a window to the world. What is different and what is the same? What do children eat in Kenya? Do the houses in a Brazilian favela look like mine? Are siblings just as annoying in Mongolia? What kind of pets do families have in Germany?

The images needn't come from another land: city kids can envision life on a farm, house dwellers can get a feeling for apartment life, those in the mountains can see life by the ocean. Beyond learning how other children live, video and animation also have the power to take us places we couldn't otherwise visit, from the depths of the ocean to the inside of the body.

The videos are only a springboard; their true value emerges in postviewing activities: pretend play, art projects, and the kind of guided reflection that contributes to lifelong media literacy. Here, too, technology can play a role, with children becoming media producers, not just consumers. They can take digital photos or videos of their own environment, share them with others, and compare how people's lives are alike and not.

Mogens Vemmer (Danish public television's former head of children's programs) is a wise man: he used to say that when children turned on the TV, they should know from the programming where they were. Vemmer's vision brought to the screen the best of good early education: a safe and solid home base from which to explore the world.

As David so eloquently shares, video can have a powerful impact in the world of learning for a child. When teachers have an awareness and knowledge of how to authentically use video to support children's learning, they can help children develop a respect for the differences that exist in our world. For example, a child can learn how other children and families value school and education when watching a video of a third-grade child in Japan attending school and tutoring programs through dinnertime.

As valuable as videos can be, it is important to keep in mind that 90 percent of children ages four to six years old engage with some sort of screen for an average of two hours a day (Rideout and Hamel 2006). Television is the most commonly practiced technology-related activity in homes across the United States (Takeuchi 2011). Remember, if you use television or videos, use them in intentional and meaningful ways. You can show children how television and videos can be used to inspire, teach, and compel us to make a difference in our world (NAEYC and FRC 2012).

DETERMINING A PLACE TO VIEW VIDEOS

Determining a space to show videos in a classroom can be difficult. Unfortunately, the location may be determined by classroom size or available resources. It is important to remember that wherever the screen is placed, a substantial number of viewers with clipboards or whiteboards are free to cluster around it to record questions and observations. When I was teaching preschool, I was lucky enough to have two large-group spaces. In one space, I had a computer monitor for viewing, and in the other space, I had a large screen that would roll down over a bulletin board. In both spaces, the screen was high enough for all children to see, and there was rug space for a large group of children to spread out and comfortably view the video.

Using Video Snapshots to Support Learning

As many early childhood educators recognize, children need concrete experiences to engage with and understand concepts. Videos provide a developmentally appropriate vehicle to access and understand concepts. Through audio and visual input, children are able to process information. It is important to note that the American Academy of Pediatrics (2011) suggests that children avoid screen time before the age of two years. Once children enter preschool, teachers can enhance their processing of new information by crafting thoughtful experiences with videos that invite them to

✓ jump-start a collaborative search,

✓ conduct research, and

✓ deepen understanding.

JUMP-START A COLLABORATIVE SEARCH

A video can provide an alternative to impossible field trips. A trip to an aquarium or nature center can be out of reach financially or geographically for some, and some programs may not be able to take field trips of any kind. Regardless of why a real field trip isn't possible, a virtual field trip through a video can be an authentic substitute. In chapters 4 and 8, I describe parts of the process of acquiring a fish for a classroom I once taught in. I told the children that as a class they would decide which fish we would get for our classroom. In our conversation, I showed them the large vase that would house the fish upon its arrival. In order to get them thinking about the types of fish, I showed them a video that explored fish of various lakes, seas, and oceans. While they watched, I invited them to draw sketches of fish they would be interested in bringing to our classroom. As the children created their sketches, they were able to process the video and the fish possibilities in their own way. After watching the video, we came together and some of the children shared their drawings while describing the fish they saw. In my observation, children retain information

more successfully if they have multiple experiences with materials. The video shown was placed in our technology center for children to view whenever they wished to revisit it. After the first large-group viewing, small groups of children visited the technology center; later, particular children visited the center to rewatch the video. In this case, the video was used to provide a powerful visual entry into a search for a fish and was also used as an ongoing search tool for small groups and individual children.

CONDUCT RESEARCH

Young children, like adults, can conduct research to learn about their own culture as well as cultures on the opposite side of the globe. In the context of early childhood, research is young children gathering knowledge and processing new information. Exploring and exposing young children to regions of the world and new cultures can be done meaningfully and authentically when children have the opportunity to conduct research in a way that activates their senses. Consider these possible ways for young children to conduct research:

- View videos.

- Observe photographs.

- Conduct interviews.

- Read books, articles, and plays.

- Act out stories and events.

- Create observational drawings.

- Sing songs.

- Explore art.

- Handle and observe artifacts.

- Try on clothing.

- Eat food.

In order to carry out such an investigation of Japanese culture, my former preschool class of children was given an opportunity to taste Japanese food, try on traditional Japanese clothing, explore Japanese art, build Japanese structures with blocks, sing Japanese songs, and of course meet people from Japan and/or people who have lived in Japan. After a couple of weeks of building

schema on Japan through these types of experiences, the children were invited to identify something they wanted to know about. The children's questions fell into three categories: buildings, food, and clothing. Based on the questions, the children were put into one of these three inquiry groups. In these inquiry groups, a teacher or classroom assistant worked with each group to explore answers to their questions using a variety of resources. During this investigation, the preschoolers worked with their sixth-grade learning partners to learn more about Japan. The sixth graders provided the preschoolers with information from reliable research resources that the sixth graders had been learning about. Among the resources available were a variety of short videos found on Safari Montage, a web-based program that offers children access to a wide variety of video clips. Teachers can create playlists specific to a certain topic for inquiry groups or individual children. Less-expensive alternatives to Safari Montage include the web-based video library on the Discovery Channel website or the PBS website.

Preschool class watches a video of a conversation between Fred Rogers and Eric Carle to start an author study of Eric Carle. (*www.redleafpress.org/tech/7-2.aspx*)

Subscribers to Safari Montage can use it to create playlists of videos by topic. While watching the videos, the children created drawings of items they noticed that might help answer their questions. And sometimes they had more questions after watching the videos. For example, a preschooler who wanted to know if people wear jeans in Japan drew a person wearing jeans after she noticed Japanese people in a video wearing jeans. In this experience, videos were used to help children answer inquiry questions. It is also important to note that in this experience, the use of videos was among one of many research tools used to support the inquiry process.

DEEPEN UNDERSTANDING

In early childhood, children learn about particular elements of the world around them. Among these elements, children learn about bodies of water such as rivers. In an investigation of rivers, children learn that rivers are home to a diverse collection of living creatures. In a kindergarten or early elementary class, children may also study how rivers in different regions are home to different living creatures. To facilitate this understanding, children could watch videos of various types of rivers around the nation or the world. The Discovery Channel website has video clips available free of charge—some of the best clips are from their *Planet Earth* series. As the children watch a collection of short videos about rivers, they can create drawings, record questions, and take notes on intriguing moments. Immediately after watching the videos, the children can turn and talk to one another about their questions or moments of amazement. In these conversations, children should be encouraged to use specific science vocabulary to articulate their observations while they develop an understanding that others have different questions or ideas about what is amazing or interesting.

More sophisticated thinking can also be prompted with videos. Using videos available on the Discovery Channel website, you can show videos describing elements of a particular food chain. In order to discuss how people can interfere with these food chains, you might show another video of individuals fishing. In this case, the videos can be used to explore both science and social concepts. Children view a video with a specific topic in mind that later provides a resource for them to refer to during focused conversations around new concepts. While watching these videos, children can also organize their observations on a T chart with words or illustrations. After recording their observations, children can discuss their findings in small groups. If this learning experience is done later in the year, you might want to extend the activity by providing the groups with an article from the magazine *Time for Kids*, which explores these similarities and differences. In these small groups, children can underline new information or learn material to support further discussion. In this experience, children view video with a high-level task and focus. After viewing the video, the children are to utilize higher-level social skills while working in small groups to further their learning independently.

Using Video Snapshots to Support Assessment

Like audio recordings, videos provide teachers with a snapshot in time that they can refer to later. Unlike audio recordings, videos can provide teachers with the ability not only to listen but also to watch children interacting with one another. Therefore, videos provide an amazing opportunity to learn about the children. When viewing recordings, teachers can watch through a particular lens. This focus provides a way to sift through all the information and evidence present in the video. Teachers can watch the same video repeatedly, viewing it with a new focus each time and coming away with a whole new set of valuable information. Teachers can use the videos to assess and learn from

✓ classroom routines to support independence and problem solving,

✓ students' classroom experiences, and

✓ effectiveness of teaching.

CLASSROOM ROUTINES TO SUPPORT INDEPENDENCE AND PROBLEM SOLVING

In early childhood classrooms, children are learning how to use language to convey thoughts, ideas, needs, and wants. They are also learning how to use words to solve social problems. In high-quality early childhood programs, there are ample opportunities for children to learn and use new emotional vocabulary words. Class meetings provide an opportunity for a whole class to come together to explore social problems that are affecting the entire class. In class meetings, there are particular roles for children. There are speakers and listeners. There might be notetakers and material managers if certain equipment, such as puppets or books, is needed to support a conversation in the meeting. These roles are all important to the success of the meeting. Sometimes the material needed in a class meeting to solve a problem is a video of the class at work during normal routines. If a new dramatic play center has opened with a limit of four visitors, a potential issue may be that children enter the center without looking to see how many children are already there. A video of the children working in the center can provide a reflective tool to help them observe moments when they can come and go without looking at how many children are already visiting the center. Observing these moments may also be a scaffolding device to help the children develop strategies or tools to solve the problem. A child may suggest to his classmates that when they arrive at the center, they should stop and count how many children are already playing. Then the teacher can help implement this strategy by suggesting a "stop-and-count line" at the entrance of the center, cueing the children to their first job before entering the center. Another child might suggest making a list of children who are interested in visiting. The teacher can help the class implement that strategy by modeling how to record each child's name on a provided clipboard. In some situations, while helping children solve social problems, a video of their own actions may be the best tool to support them in identifying solutions to classroom issues.

STUDENTS' CLASSROOM EXPERIENCES

Teachers can use video all sorts of ways to capture various learning experiences in the classroom. Capturing these experiences—and later, reviewing them—can be extremely informative. For example, you can videotape a large-group read-aloud and later review it to analyze the types of questions asked of the children, the responses of the children, the pace of the read-aloud, and the overall engagement of the children. Use the Recorded Learning Experience Reflection Sheet (form 7-1) while viewing your videos to support and guide reflection. Viewing yourself in action can help you determine

7.1 Recorded Learning Experience Reflection Sheet

Children Present: Mark	Date: 1/20/11

Learning Experience: Large group read-aloud during morning meeting

Materials Used: *Violet's Music* by Angela Johnson

Goals/Objectives: Appreciating music anywhere we go

Evidence of meeting or not meeting objectives:
While reading the story, I asked, "Has anyone here made their own instrument and enjoyed playing it as much as Violet does here in the story?" Three kids raised their hands and shared their stories of making an instrument.

Questions/observations made by children:
"How did Violet make that horn?"
"Can we make our own instruments today?"

Skills particular children may need additional experiences with:
Skills: None   Children: None

Notes for future teaching:
Open a "special interest art center" for the rest of the week with interesting art supplies that can be used to make instruments.

Christine Caro Bowie, second-grade teacher, reflects on using videos to support learning. (*www.redleafpress.org/tech/7-3.aspx*)

if certain concepts need to be revisited or skipped. You can also identify certain groups of children that may need additional support to develop particular skills or concepts.

EFFECTIVENESS OF TEACHING

It is important to remember that technology can be used to assess not only children, but also your own practices in particular routines or learning experiences. Videotaping yourself leading a large- or small-group learning experience can be an amazing reflective tool to refine your teaching practices. For example, when introducing new math concepts, you need to ensure that children use and understand new vocabulary. Teachers can record themselves working with small groups and later review the recordings to determine the use of new vocabulary. In this review, teachers would be able to identify which children are using what words and whether they are using them appropriately.

Using Video Snapshots to Exhibit Learning

Young children do not necessarily have the vocabulary and metacognitive skills to articulate their learning processes to others. Using videos to describe and exhibit learning processes is an amazing way to show parents and other professionals what a child has learned in a particular experience or over a period of time. Oftentimes, others can learn the most about children when these videos are paired with your descriptions or a conversation with the parent or other professional about the skills or concepts being exhibited. Teachers can share learning when using video snapshots to

- ✓ share dramatic play and storytelling,
- ✓ demonstrate learning over time, and
- ✓ show understanding of science concepts.

SHARE DRAMATIC PLAY AND STORYTELLING

In early childhood classrooms, children are learning to take on the roles of others through dramatic play centers and to solve problems through discussion. Teachers can support this development by providing opportunities to dramatize stories. The effort that children put into these experiences and the learning that takes place can be substantial and can be captured through videotaping them. Teachers can use these videos to exhibit what children have learned through the process. DVDs often include segments with commentary over scenes. In these videos, viewers learn background information about how a certain scene or effect was made possible. A similar strategy can be used within a video to highlight learning by using movie-making software such as iMovie, Windows Movie Maker, or Windows Live Movie Maker. You import the movie, then add audio tracks with your commentary on particular skills or concepts being developed in the experience. Share this video by uploading it to your classroom website for family members and other visitors to watch and learn from. If a classroom website is not available, you can burn the video to a DVD that families can check out and take home to view.

DEMONSTRATE LEARNING OVER TIME

Video clips taken throughout an investigation can be pulled together in a compilation video to demonstrate learning. For example, when a teacher jump-starts an inquiry unit on magnets, he videotapes children talking about questions they have about magnets. Throughout this investigation, he continues to record particular moments when children are conducting research and finding answers to their inquiry questions. After the investigation is finished, he can create a video compilation with clips of children posing their questions and then providing the answers to their questions, which they found as they researched and experimented with magnets. Or in a preschool investigation of the growth of plants, each child plants a seed in a pot. Each day, a different child is named "Botanical Scientist." The botanical scientist is responsible

Some schools or programs celebrate learning in the area of science and other disciplines by hosting celebration events where families are invited to come visit classrooms and children describe what they have learned. However, young children, particularly in preschool and kindergarten, are still in the early stages of developing language and feeling confidence to speak publicly on a focused topic. In these cases, showing videos of the children describing their processes and learning, recorded earlier, provides an opportunity for children to share their learning without having to share it live and publicly.

for observing the pots and drawing his or her observations. Over time, the children learn that plant growth is a slow process, and in order to nurture that process, plants need consistent, gentle care. As the children observe, draw, and speak about their observations, their teacher takes photographs, video, and audio clips. At the end of the investigation, the teacher compiles a video to show families that the children are able to slowly grasp concepts related to plant care and growth.

SHOW UNDERSTANDING OF SCIENCE CONCEPTS

Steve Spangler of www.stevespanglerscience.com and Science Bob of www .sciencebob.com provide videos of various science experiments to educate children and adults on how materials in science can create certain phenomena or react with each other in surprising ways. Children can learn the format of

describing and conducting an experiment for an audience. In helping children learn this format, a teacher may elaborate on how a scientist describes what she is going to do and how the scientist acknowledges what people think the result of the experiment may be. The teacher can also highlight that after completing an experiment, a scientist can elaborate on the scientific principles involved as a way to further educate viewers. Working individually or in small groups, children can take on the role of a scientist by becoming particularly familiar with a certain experiment so they can replicate it for viewers. The teacher can then record the experiments while the scientists—the children—adhere to the experiment description format they learned. Finally, the teacher can compile these videos and post them to a classroom website where visitors can view and learn about particular experiments.

◆　　◆　　◆

Discussing and reading about new ideas is important so children can process and understand information; however, when children view videos, they are given a glimpse at a moment in time. Viewing videos of concepts provides a structure with which to understand. This structure allows children to construct questions and understanding as prior knowledge is applied. Videos provide children with a high-quality and meaningful opportunity to authentically explore new ideas at a pace unique to the child. Like photographs, videos provide an authentic research tool that young children can use to gather information and foster a sense of inquiry.

» TOOLBOX TIPS

IDENTIFYING VIDEO RESOURCES

There are a variety of video resources available online that teachers can use to enhance classroom units and investigations. Consider these possible resources as a starting place for implementation.

RESOURCE	ACCESS	WEBSITE
YouTube*	Free	www.youtube.com
TeacherTube	Free	www.teachertube.com
SAFARI Montage*	Subscription	www.safarimontage.com
BrainPOP*	Subscription	www.brainpop.com
BrainPOP Jr.	Subscription	www.brainpopjr.com
PBS*	Free	pbs.org
PBS Kids*	Free	pbskids.org
National Geographic*	Free	nationalgeographic.com
National Geographic Kids*	Free	kids.nationalgeographic.com
Discovery*	Free	dsc.discovery.com

* indicates an available iPad application to access web-based videos

While searching for videos in these programs, it is important to ask yourself the following questions:

- Is the length of this video appropriate for the group that will be viewing it?

- Can the length be shortened if it is too long for this group?

- Does the video address the concepts or essential understandings of the unit or investigation?

- Where does this video fit into the learning sequence?

- What would be the best format (large-group or small-group) for the children to view the video?

- What preparations (downloading, syncing, setup, takedown, or collaboration) do I need to consider to offer the viewing of this video?

If you ask yourself these questions while reviewing potential videos, you will make a thoughtful and informed decision on the most appropriate use of videos.

Some resources require classroom or school subscriptions in order to access available videos. Some district or school networks may restrict access to certain websites, such as youtube.com and teachertube.com, so it is important to explore the extent of connectivity and restrictions before planning particular learning experiences using these resources. The resources above are intended to provide teachers with knowledge of available resources to acquire videos for their classroom, while at the same time considering costs and common limitations in educational settings.

Forms

7.1 Recorded Learning Experience Reflection Sheet

www.redleafpress.org/tech/7-1.pdf

7.1 Recorded Learning Experience Reflection Sheet

Children Present:

Date:

Learning Experience:

Materials Used:

Goals/Objectives:

Evidence of meeting or not meeting objectives:

Questions/observations made by children:

Skills particular children may need additional experiences with:

Skills:

Children:

Notes for future teaching:

8
Multi-Touch Mobile Devices Bring the World to Our Fingertips

www.redleafpress.org/tech/8-1.aspx

Mr. Elliott:	All right, boys and girls, you should be just about finished cleaning up your art materials. Once you have your materials cleaned up, take out your book club books.
Arnav:	What? Mr. Elliott, I am not finished with my sculpture. I need to keep working. I am not ready to clean up.
Mr. Elliott:	Arnav, it is time to move on to our book club groups to discuss what we have read so far. You need to begin putting your materials away until tomorrow.
Arnav:	But, Mr. Elliott, I am not ready to!

Second-grade teacher Mr. Elliott noticed that Arnav was having trouble transitioning from activity to activity throughout the day. Arnav is diagnosed with a high-functioning form of autism and sees Mrs. Jordan, the school learning resource teacher, regularly. Mr. Elliott discussed his observations with Mrs. Jordan, and together they explored ideas to help Arnav with transitions throughout the day. In their search for possible strategies, Mrs. Jordan mentioned trying an iPad application called First Then Visual Schedule by Good Karma Applications, Inc., which she had heard about in a workshop a few weeks before. Both Mr. Elliott and Mrs. Jordan acquired the application and learned its features. They learned that the application allowed users to create schedules unique to individuals and that these schedules could be displayed in a variety of ways, each with visual and audio cues. They were especially impressed by the ability to use their own photos in the schedules. Both Mr. Elliott and Mrs. Jordan sat down with Arnav and told him what they had found and how they thought it would help him. The three of them took photographs of important parts of the classroom or school to help remind him of upcoming events or activities throughout the day. The application allowed Arnav to see and hear his daily schedule. Arnav was reminded about what activities would come next and could mentally prepare for the transition. Mr. Elliott noticed a quick change in Arnav's ability to transition between activities. A couple of weeks later, Mr. Elliott and Mrs. Jordan sat down with Arnav to talk with him about how the application was helping him throughout the day. Arnav had also noticed a change in his ability to move through activities, and overall he enjoyed school more.

With the invention of multi-touch mobile devices, technology in the lives of millions of people across the world has changed drastically. In 2010, a Futuresource Consulting report predicted that by 2013, one billion people will own smartphones. Never before has information been so available or has communication been so instant. Multi-touch mobile devices are now among the many resources individuals can use to learn about the world around them. Those who have an iPhone or smartphone can use Yelp to look up restaurants in a particular neighborhood with a touch of a few buttons. They can use the SoundHound application for a smart device to find the title and artist of a song playing nearby. Children growing up in this technology-driven world are accustomed to the immediacy of answers and content. It's critical that classrooms connect to the outside world and that teachers construct learning experiences that make the best use of the technology available. Children can lose interest or fail to take in new knowledge if answers are not sought after in the moment. Multi-touch mobile devices offer educators another tool to enhance curriculum and address early learning standards (Couse and Chen 2010). Just as teachers plan meaningful learning experiences with manipulatives to address a mathematics concept, they can also use various multi-touch mobile device applications to address mathematics concepts. Chapter 9 discusses how teachers can identify certain instructional strategies that include technology and insert them into curriculum maps where appropriate. In the classroom, it is imperative that experiences with technology, such as multi-touch mobile devices, are used in a thoughtful fashion. Planning and implementation should be relevant to the content and material children are learning in the classroom (Chiong and Shuler 2010).

» TOOLBOX TIP

SELECTING THE BEST MULTI-TOUCH MOBILE DEVICE

More than fifteen different tablet computers are available to consumers today. Among these are the Acer Iconia, Motorola Xoom, Samsung Galaxy Tab 10.1, BlackBerry PlayBook, and most notably, Apple's iPad. All of these tablet computers operate on one of four commonly used operating systems: Android, iOS, Windows, and BlackBerry. These devices have opened many doors to learners of all ages, and new doors are opened each day.

With the wide variety and ever-increasing number of choices, teachers and administrators need to consider the following questions to determine which devices are best for their school or program:

- What are the majority of computers used at the school or center (PC or Apple)?

- What ages or grade levels will be using these devices?

- Are there particular disciplines for which the devices will be used most?
- What is a running list of potential applications to use on this device?
- How many devices do you intend to acquire?
- What is the current budget?
- Are there any grants available to possibly increase the budget?
- Does your district/school/center have any vendors that may provide a discount for buying in bulk?
- Are there opportunities to lease this equipment?
- What technology skills do the staff currently have?
- Is there a designated individual to conduct ongoing research in applications, organization, and deployment of the devices?
- Are there opportunities for professional development to educate staff and faculty on how to use one of these devices?
- Is there a secure place to store these devices?

Each program is going to arrive at the best device based on the uniqueness of its situation. The consideration of these questions is critical. In times when budget is the primary determinant for acquiring technology equipment, high levels of thought need to be evident in the proposal and planning for such technology. Managing the planning and implementation of this technology is easiest when done in a team, whether this includes another teacher, a technology coordinator, or parent or community volunteers.

Introducing Multi-Touch Mobile Devices to Children

Obtaining multi-touch mobile devices can be extremely exciting, and eagerness to get them into the children's hands can be overwhelming. To be sure the equipment is well taken care of and used properly, it is important to carefully plan how you will begin using the devices in your classroom. Children come to your classroom with a range of experiences with multi-touch mobile devices: some will have never seen one before, and some may use one at their own home on a daily basis. These experiences are critical in how and when you introduce ideas, skills, and concepts related to multi-touch mobile devices.

The next few pages provide an outline for introducing the devices and the applications the children will be using. They also provide baseline recommended timelines for when you may want to consider introducing experiences or reviewing previous learning using multi-touch mobile devices.

INTRODUCING MULTI-TOUCH MOBILE DEVICES TO ALL AGES

When introducing multi-touch mobile devices, it is important to discuss some key elements. The Multi-Touch Mobile Device Introduction Map below can help guide you into a thoughtful and intentional introduction to these devices. It is important to note that each group of children is different, so please use this in the way that best fits your class. Perhaps your introduction can be done in one sitting, while other teachers will need to spread out the introduction over two or three sessions.

Multi-Touch Mobile Device Introduction Map

Discuss Physical Features: Shape, Weight, Look, Feel

What do you think is inside?

Why do you think it is so heavy?

Discuss Device Parts: Screen, Buttons, Headphone Jack, Volume (and Any Other Parts)

Discuss the functions of these parts.

Tell how to care for these parts.

Pose questions to the group:

Have you seen one of these before? If so, where?

Who was using it?

What were they doing with it?

How do you think this works with only a few buttons?

Model Simple Navigation

Turn it on.

Discuss the difference between swiping and scrolling.

Model swiping and scrolling.

Discuss applications.

INTRODUCING MULTI-TOUCH MOBILE DEVICE APPLICATIONS TO ALL AGES

It is important to introduce multi-touch mobile device applications just as thoughtfully as you would introduce the multi-touch mobile device itself. Use the Introducing Multi-Touch Mobile Device Application Map below as a guide to carrying out an intentional application introduction. Like introducing the multi-touch mobile device experience(s), you need to consider your group's current knowledge and development to determine the best way to introduce the applications. With applications, you may be able to introduce an application in one sitting, while others will need to spread the introduction over two or three sessions.

Introducing Multi-Touch Mobile Device Application Map

Refer to previous learning experience or familiar concept.
Acknowledge how children will build on that using a multi-touch mobile device application.
Introduce the application.

Title
Location on screen (location in folder, if applicable)
Icon image

Walk through the application.

Model what children will do.
Discuss task (done with independence or with teacher support).

Child models for the rest of the class.

Find and opening application.
Navigate the application.
Model the task for the day within the application.

Review any navigation skills the group is working on.

Scrolling
Swiping
Holding
Carrying
Retrieving/storing
Taking home/bringing back to school

INTRODUCING MULTI-TOUCH MOBILE DEVICES TO PRESCHOOL AND KINDERGARTEN CHILDREN

These two levels are kept together because children in preschool and kindergarten are learning how to do school. Preschool and kindergarten teachers must be extra careful in introducing classroom materials. A multi-touch mobile device is another classroom material and should be introduced like any other classroom material.

EXPERIENCE	MONTH
Introduction to multi-touch mobile devices	September
Introduction to facilitated small-group work with multi-touch mobile devices	October
Introduction to independent use of multi-touch mobile devices under supervision	April

INTRODUCING MULTI-TOUCH MOBILE DEVICES TO FIRST-GRADE STUDENTS

Schools have begun adopting one-to-one multi-touch mobile device programs. If your school adopts a one-to-one program, it is important to provide orientation sessions for families as well as the children. Multi-touch mobile devices need just as much thought and care in their deployment as laptop computers.

In first grade, children have developed better eye-hand coordination and motor-planning abilities, so it is appropriate to introduce them to holding and carrying multi-touch mobile devices. The gradual introduction to experiences is still important at this age, so children should have ample time to develop an understanding of how to engage with the multi-touch mobile devices in particular ways.

EXPERIENCE	MONTH
Introduction to multi-touch mobile devices	September
Introduction to facilitated small-group work with multi-touch mobile devices	October
Introduction to independent use of multi-touch mobile devices under supervision	November
Introduction to holding the devices	November
Introduction to carrying the devices	January

INTRODUCING MULTI-TOUCH MOBILE DEVICES TO SECOND-GRADE STUDENTS

Experiences in second grade can be introduced more quickly because children this age are better able to retain ideas and apply them to experiences. It is still important, however, to observe how the children are engaging with the multi-touch mobile devices to determine if adjustments need to be made to the timeline of introducing experience.

EXPERIENCE	MONTH
Introduction to multi-touch mobile devices	Early September
Introduction to facilitated small-group work with multi-touch mobile devices	Late September
Introduction to holding and carrying multi-touch mobile devices	October
Introduction to independent use with teacher support	January

INTRODUCING MULTI-TOUCH MOBILE DEVICES TO THIRD-GRADE STUDENTS

Children seven and eight years old are developing the ability to apply ideas and concepts to various contexts, so opportunities to take multi-touch mobile devices home to use are appropriate at this age. This may not be an option for all schools and communities, but it is an option to be considered.

EXPERIENCE	MONTH
Introduction to multi-touch mobile devices	Early September
Introduction to facilitated small-group work with multi-touch mobile devices	Late September
Introduction to holding and carrying multi-touch mobile devices	October
Introduction to independent use with teacher support	January
Introduction to multi-touch mobile devices use at home	February
Introduction to borrowing multi-touch mobile devices for use at home	March

» **TOOLBOX TIPS**

COMPARING TABLET COMPUTERS

Choosing a tablet that meets the needs of particular programs can be difficult. There are, however, a few resources that can help teachers and administrators determine the best choice for their program. These comparison resources list specific features, costs, and operating systems, as well as reviews on each of the devices.

TITLE	WEBSITE
Tablet PC Comparison	www.tabletpccomparison.net
Cnet Reviews	http://reviews.cnet.com/tablets
PC Mag	www.pcmag.com
Tablet PC Review	www.tabletpcreview.com
Tablet PC Comparisons	www.tabletpc2.com/Compare.htm

Using Multi-Touch Mobile Devices to Support Learning

Today, multi-touch mobile devices offer teachers the ability to make any moment a teachable moment, anytime, anywhere. Andrew Beights, a technology specialist, joined a group of first graders on a field trip to an apple orchard. On the bus, he used the application StoryBuddy by Tapfuze to collect children's background knowledge on apples. After being provided a question, the children were able to answer by drawing an illustration and/or writing text. On the bus ride back, Andrew was able to revisit the children's ideas to see if they had changed over the course of the day, given what they had learned at the orchard. There are multiple ways you can use these devices to enhance learning experiences and engage children with an unlimited number of concepts.

Teachers can help children use multi-touch mobile devices to

✓ facilitate conversation while observing photographs,

✓ engage with literature,

✓ develop skills in music,

✓ inspire creation in the arts,

✓ support brainstorming,

✓ create video books, and

✓ conduct research.

FACILITATE CONVERSATION WHILE OBSERVING PHOTOGRAPHS

Multi-touch mobile devices such as the Apple iPad or iPad2 can be used to support high-level conversations when working with children in small groups. As chapter 2 describes, photographs offer teachers and young children the opportunity to observe and talk about the world around them. The iPad, as well as other mobile devices, can house a vast number of photos, providing opportunities for discussion just a few finger swipes away. After syncing them to an iPad, photos can easily be organized into album folders using an application like Photo-Sort by Romain Henry or Sort Shots.

When it's time to look at a group of photographs with the children, simply choose the album created for a particular learning experience and begin browsing. For example, if a preschool class is about to embark on an investigation of various parks in the community, the teacher may take a variety of photographs of these parks to house in an album for the children to review. While reviewing the photographs, the children can identify similarities and differences between parks, share stories of visits they have had to parks, or identify any pieces of equipment that appear unfamiliar. In these conversations, the teacher can gather valuable information about children's level of interest, background knowledge, and types of questions to explore in the upcoming investigation. You might ask, Why not simply show children printed photographs rather than on an iPad? You should still show children printed photographs and provide magnifying glasses to take a close look. You should also use multi-touch mobile devices to show children photographs, because you show them one of the many ways we can use these devices. Using these devices also facilitates on-the-spot learning experiences. For example, if a class is outside noticing the differences between the leaves that have fallen on the ground, the teacher can use an iPad to quickly take snapshots of the leaves, which can immediately be reviewed in small groups indoors.

Providing a variety of opportunities with photographs can further support children's learning of particular concepts (Wellings and Levine 2009). A teacher could first show the children the photographs they took outside in a whole-group setting. Then she could invite small groups to a table to discuss the photographs. After concluding the small-group conversations, the teacher could place the iPad in a science center for curious children to revisit on their own time. In these situations, teachers have multiple opportunities to gather information about a child's background knowledge on a given set of concepts. The At-a-Glance Background Knowledge Assessment (form 2.2) and the Individual Background Knowledge Assessment (form 2.3) described in chapter 2 can be helpful in assessing children's background knowledge as they review photographs on a multi-touch mobile device.

ENGAGE WITH LITERATURE

In classrooms, children engage with high-quality literature, traditionally in the form of books. With the invention of multi-touch mobile devices, children—and adults—have access to books in another way. Today, adults can be found reading and scrolling through e-books on their iPads or an e-reader, such as a Nook or Kindle, in homes, libraries, cabs, airports, bus stops, and clinic waiting rooms. As adults continue to model reading in this sort of way, teachers of very young children will soon see children pick up blocks and pretend to read as if using an e-reader. They will see children finger swipe the blocks up and down and side to side, as if they are scrolling through pages.

Chapter 4 discussed how One More Story can be used to enhance a listening center through providing audio and visual experiences with children's literature. Digital books for multi-touch mobile devices such as the iPad provide a similar but mobile experience. When children view digital books as applications, they can engage with the content, vocabulary, and characters in a whole new way. The application That's Not JUNK HD by Kiwa Media provides teachers with the opportunity to allow children to hear a fluent reader read a story to them. You can also remove the audio reading and record yourself as you read the story. When using this application with preschool and kindergarten children, teachers can record conversations around each page. Children in first through third grade can make their own recordings, and they can listen to

It is important to be thoughtful about how you introduce digital books, especially if children have not seen them before. Children understand new concepts more successfully when the concepts are introduced in a familiar context. Many of Dr. Seuss's books are familiar to young children. Therefore the Dr. Seuss e-books are an appropriate way to move children toward the idea of enjoying and reading a text as an e-book as well as a printed book. When introducing e-books, it's important to carefully model how to navigate the app or e-book. After the children have observed you and have had the opportunity to try one out under supervision, they will develop the ability to work with multi-touch mobile devices independently. With practice and patient instruction, young children will be able to interact with e-books in small groups without your assistance.

their reading played back to them. The recordings can also be played back for a group or for the whole class after hooking up an iPad 2 to an LCD projector or placing a first-generation iPad under a document camera. You can also review the recordings to identify any children who may need additional experiences with particular skills or concepts. Assessment tools for using recordable digital books are discussed later in the chapter.

DEVELOP SKILLS IN MUSIC

Multi-touch mobile devices can support exploration of the arts as well. In chapter 4, various ways to support music-skill development using audio recordings were suggested. Brigid Finucane, a music teacher for Merit School of Music in Chicago, uses multi-touch mobile devices to support young children in their development of particular skills. One of the national music standards that Brigid uses calls for children to sing alone and with others. She begins teaching this by introducing the concepts of solo, duet, trio, and quartet. She then invites the children to try singing in these different-sized groups by echoing a tune she models for them. Brigid uses a recording application such as Recorder HD by Decipher Media or One Tap Voice Memos by 1to1class.com (available for the iPad) to capture her recordings. These applications have an option to export and e-mail audio files. This allows Brigid to send files to herself for later review, to family members to celebrate particular milestones, and to other teachers to help them better understand where the children are with particular skills.

Karla Beard-Leroy, music teacher, uses an iPad to show a second-grade class a video to support steady beats and multicultural studies. (*www .redleafpress.org/tech/8-2.aspx*)

Brigid also looks for ways to support children in developing their listening skills and ability to identify the different sounds made by various instruments. With a limited budget, she is not able to acquire and share all the instruments she would like. Instead, she has begun to develop a library of applications that depict the sound of various instruments, such as a xylophone, electric drum, bongo drum, Autoharp, piano, guitar, and washboard. The iPad allows her students to hear and become familiar with a wide variety of instruments.

INSPIRE CREATION IN THE ARTS

Multi-touch mobile devices can provide children with opportunities to be inspired and carry out their creativity. The MoMA AB EX NY (Museum of Modern Art *Abstract Expressionist New York*) application by the Museum of Modern Art can help children learn about the works of famous artists. This application houses the collections of various artists and allows users to zoom in to many of the pieces. The application has several videos of interviews with individuals who are familiar with the perspective and intentions of the artists. There are also several videos that can provide children with the opportunity to see demonstrations of artistic styles and techniques. A classroom or art teacher can project one of these videos to exhibit a particular style or technique that will be tried that day. The videos, which provide details about particular artists, can be an incredible resource for a class venturing on an artist study. The combination of actual pieces of art, in-depth information about artists, and videos that show individuals how certain styles can be replicated and can inspire children to explore art in new ways.

When searching through applications, be sure to review what devices the applications are intended for. Applications made for the iPhone can be expanded to fit the screen on an iPad, as seen in this photograph of the I Spy Riddle Race application.

SUPPORT BRAINSTORMING

Chapters 4 and 7 included a description of how a science center was used in my preschool classroom to help the children think about what it means to have a pet fish in the classroom. Among the many materials and resources available to the children, an iPad that housed an application called HD Marine

197

In addition to picture books, author studies, and alphabet puzzles, there are many creative ways to supporting children's early writing development. Encourage children to write reminder notes for the class, provide stationery for children to write letters to family members, or arrange for less-structured activities in a writing center. Children can make books about topics of their choosing. In a writing center, children may be able to make books with various-sized paper stapled together. Technology can also be one tool among these resources. You can show children how they can publish books using applications on an iPad or other tablet. Cumulatively, these activities make children aware that people write for a variety of reasons. Children will begin to understand that they are each on their own journey of learning to write.

Life by ImagineThis was included. This application contains a variety of photographs and descriptions of tropical fish. The children were able to view these photographs independently and at their own pace. As the children browsed the photographs and discovered a fish they were interested in having in the classroom, they made an observational drawing and tucked it into a research folder. As a class, we periodically reviewed the folder to become updated on the class's developing ideas.

CREATE VIDEO BOOKS

Chapter 6 discussed how David Curry helped his students to publish video books using computer software programs. Children can also use multi-touch mobile devices to create and publish their own video books. Draw for iPad by Erica Sadun, Drawing Pad by Darren Murtha Design, and SonicPics by Humble Daisy are iPad applications that provide the opportunity for children to easily develop their own video books. Children can use the Draw application to create colorful illustrations for the front cover, pages, and back cover of their books. With the help of a teacher or classroom volunteer, the pages can be

imported into the SonicPics application, where the adult and children can work together to arrange the pages in the sequence desired. The children can then record the telling of the story as they flip through the pages with a swipe of a finger. The video book can be exported to e-mail or sent to YouTube or a particular computer. In helping children develop confidence in themselves as readers and writers, teachers can provide opportunities for children to share books they have written. In these moments, children can take the opportunity to read or share their electronically written video book with the class. Afterward, the rest of the class can ask the author questions to understand the process, comprehend the story, or perhaps develop new ideas for their own writing. In this process, the experience of creating and publishing video books using technology is woven into daily routines. Children arrive at the understanding that among their classroom materials used to publish and share, such as paper, pencils, markers, paint, and scissors, there is also an iPad. This helps children begin to understand at an early age that books can be published and shared in many ways.

> When children share their published work with the class, they can share handwritten books, electronically written books, artwork using art center materials, electronically created artwork, and electronically recorded audiobooks. The variety of what children can share expands when they have the opportunity to use many technologies.

CONDUCT RESEARCH

As mentioned in chapter 7, even in preschool, children can begin to develop a concept of what it means to conduct research. In preschool and kindergarten, children learn possible ways to gather information. In primary grades, children learn how to be more intentional with the resources they use to gather information. In addition to using books, videos, photographs, and people, children need to learn simple ways to use technology to conduct research and learn about the world. In preschool and kindergarten, children make observations about weather and simple weather patterns. For example, children living in Minneapolis are able to predict cold temperatures and snow for January and February. They learn that they wear certain clothing to protect themselves from the cold weather. Meanwhile, children living in Cairns, Queensland, in Australia, learn to expect particular weather patterns for January and February as well—warm temperatures and sunshine. They also learn that they need to wear particular clothing that protects them from the hot weather. Regardless of location, children anywhere can use technology to learn about these weather patterns. The applications AccuWeather and The Weather Channel can help children learn about weather patterns in a particular area. Moreover, children can use these applications to learn about what is expected to happen for the rest of the day and the days to come. They can also use these applications to learn about severe weather to be aware of during the day or the days to come. As children become familiar with weather patterns, they begin to understand the relationship between the patterns and temperatures. For example, a child living in Milwaukee, Wisconsin, learns that a typical high temperature for the month of January is 29 degrees, while a typical temperature for the month of June is around 75 degrees. During these learning experiences, vocabulary specific to weather becomes embedded in their observations and discussions about the weather.

Carli McKenney, preschool teacher, reflects on using iPads with other resources to support children's developing research skills. (*www .redleafpress.org/tech/8-3.aspx*)

Each year, first-grade teacher Maria Larios guides her students on an exciting investigation of dinosaurs. Through collaborative efforts with her grade-level partner to search for meaningful and exciting research tools for their students to use, they discovered an additional resource application available for the iPad. The application Dinosaur!! from Halcyon Creations provides children with detailed illustrations of dinosaurs paired with known facts. Maria found this application to be particularly helpful in the middle stages of the inquiry unit, when children were actively seeking answers to the questions they had developed about the dinosaurs they chose to research. After learning about their dinosaurs using the Dinosaur application and other resources such as books, videos, and photographs of skeletons, the children choose ways to publish or present their learning. Some children take their learning and create a nonfiction big book providing facts and illustrations about particular dinosaurs. Within this learning sequence, technology is a single tool among many to facilitate and encourage inquiry.

Using Multi-Touch Mobile Devices to Support Assessment

Multi-touch mobile devices provide teachers with a multitude of ways to gather, organize, and reflect on children's progress and development. In the past, teachers have had to lug large, heavy crates to and from their homes to review workbooks, work samples, and portfolios. Never before has it been easier for teachers to carry so much valuable information in something as small as an iPad or other tablet. Several applications are available to teachers to assess

✓ literacy development and comprehension,

✓ classroom experiences throughout the disciplines, and

✓ children's knowledge of story elements.

LITERACY DEVELOPMENT AND COMPREHENSION

As more children's books are also published digitally, there is an increasingly popular option for readers to record their own readings of a story. When an e-book application offers this option, teachers can save recordings for later review to assess development of literacy skill. Some e-book applications even allow users to save multiple recordings for later review. If this option is available for

8.1 Digital Book Recording Assessment Checklist for Prereaders		
Child(ren): **Col**	Date: **12/15/10**	
Digital Book: *That's Not Junk!* by Nikki Slade Robinson		
Skill:	Yes	No
Discusses author and illustrator roles	X	
Poses questions about text	X	
Makes observations from illustrations	X	
Begins to make inferences	X	
Makes text-to-self connections	X	
Makes text-to-text connections	X	
Poses predictions	X	
Notes for Future Learning Experiences: Col appeared interested in the book; he pointed out several items he noticed. In the next book we read together, I will need to model asking questions. I may also use the recording feature of this application and have an older child read it, while asking himself or herself questions as they read to model that practice for Col. We can then listen to it together, and then record us reading it together and asking questions as we read. We can then listen to our reading, paying attention to the questions we asked.		

a particular e-book app, it can be chosen when opening up the application settings. In preschool, a teacher can listen for relevant conversations about the content of the book. A child in preschool might also announce observations or ask questions regarding the content of illustrations in the book. As children's skills improve, they might begin to point out letters or words they recognize, and soon they are able to read particular sentences from the story while paying closer attention to punctuation. The Digital Book Recording Assessment Checklists for Prereaders and Readers (forms 8.1 and 8.2) can be used to reflect on a child's interaction with concepts in books and developing literacy skills. Using these checklists periodically over time can show you how a child is increasingly able to engage with text and literacy skills.

8.2 Digital Book Recording Assessment Checklist for Readers		
Child(ren): Lee	Date: 3/17/11	
Digital Book: Memoirs of a Goldfish		
Skills:	Yes	No
Recognizes known letters	X	
Recognizes familiar sight words	X	
Makes text-to-world connections	X	
Discusses inferences using background knowledge and text	X	
Reflects on predictions		X
Creates new predictions while continuing to read	X	
Employs comprehension strategies independently to understand text	X	
Discusses author's style of writing	X	

Notes for Future Learning Experiences:

In my next read-aloud with Lee, I need to model how to reflect on my own predictions. In a large or small group read-aloud, I need to invite some children to try it out as well.

CLASSROOM EXPERIENCES THROUGHOUT THE DISCIPLINES

There are various applications available for multi-touch mobile devices that allow teachers to manipulate documents by adding text boxes, drawing, and highlighting. The TakeNotes application by Tipirneni Software, available for the iPad, allows teachers to collect data from planned and spontaneous observations of classroom routines and activities. You can view a tutorial for this application at www.padnotesapp.com. With this application, you can import your class list as a template for simple observations. Then, over time, you can gather a substantial amount of data about a child's abilities and work habits. In the observation checklist shown here, a preschool teacher observed children's ability to engage with books utilizing basic book-handling skills. In the assessment, all children were engaging with books using basic book-handling skills for a substantial period of time, ten to fifteen minutes. Notice the note to hold a class meeting to celebrate this accomplishment. The next day, in order to look at consistency with this skill, the teacher used the same assessment and noticed that a considerably smaller number of children were exhibiting this skill. The teacher acknowledged the variance in his observation at that day's class meeting. In a kindergarten classroom, a teacher can observe whether a pair of children are able to maintain focus on a given task. In a first-grade classroom, a teacher can observe whether a child has attempted a skill taught in a day's mini-lesson. In a second- or third-grade classroom, where children are working in small groups, a teacher might circulate and gather quick notes about collaborative skills evident in the group work.

You can also gather and organize anecdotal notes on children using various productivity applications available for multi-touch mobile devices. Using the TakeNotes application developed by Tipirneni Software, LLC, the checklist shown was used to conduct a quick, spontaneous observation during a self-selected center time in a preschool classroom. This same checklist was used the next day during the same time period, and the teacher's observations were very different from the day before. The teacher then facilitated a class meeting to explore what he was observing.

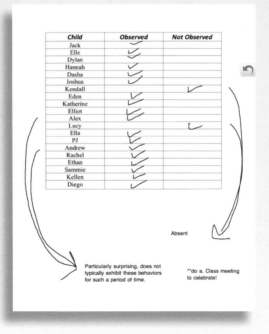

203

The PaperDesk by Web Spinner application, available for the iPad, allows teachers to create an individual folder for each child, to which anecdotal notes can be recorded and saved. You can type, write, and draw within your notes. While doing so, you can also capture an audio recording of a conversation with a child. These audio recordings are stored within the folders among the notes. With two touches on the iPad, you can be in a child's folder, reviewing and listening to previous notes. When I taught preschool, I would lie down on the floor next to a child who was making a book. With the iPad, I could record a conversation with that child about the book. In a second- or third-grade classroom, a teacher can record a writing conference with a child. In this conference, the teacher can capture goals for future writing pieces. These audio recordings can be shared with the children to listen to later independently for future support in their writing development. The teacher can take anecdotal notes or notes for future learning experiences for a child. Using PaperDesk allows teachers and other professionals to easily export and share their notes and audio files with one another. The PaperDesk application can also be used to help you organize your anecdotal notes for online database assessment systems such as Teaching Strategies GOLD.

CHILDREN'S KNOWLEDGE OF STORY ELEMENTS

In a first-grade classroom, children are learning about story events with a high level of explicitness. Andy Russell, cofounder of Launchpad Toys (introduced in chapter 1), wanted to create an application that allowed children to utilize their imaginations, along with their knowledge of basic story events and concepts, to create and animate cartoons. Launchpad Toys' application Toontastic provides children with a variety of ways to demonstrate knowledge while using their interests and imagination. Toontastic invites users to choose premade characters or to develop characters from scratch, using basic drawing tools. Users can also choose premade setting scenes or create their own. After creating the characters and pages, users can animate the pages and add varying volume-level audio tracks to accompany a particular scene to trigger emotion and feeling. Toontastic supports even the earliest learners of story events by walking them through each step of the process. After animation and audio recording is complete, you can help children export their cartoons to share with others. Cartoons can be shared with a whole class while playing them under a document camera or hooked up to an LCD projector. After

8.3 Cartoon Event Checklist

Child(ren): April		Date: 10/27/11	

Cartoon Title: The Story of My Brother Jacob

Plot:		Yes	No
Basic plot for characters and setting		X	
Setting:			
Logical for chosen plot		X	
Consistent throughout story when necessary		X	
Changes throughout story when necessary		X	
Characters:			
Logical characters for chosen plot		X	
Logical characters for chosen setting		X	
Problem:			
Logical problem for chosen characters		X	
Logical problem for chosen setting		X	
Resolution:			
Logical resolution for chosen characters		X	
Logical resolution for chosen problem		X	

Notes for Future Learning Experiences:
April put a well-developed animated cartoon together that showed how her brother Jacob once bought a pet from the pet store without talking to their parents about it first. The events of the story — going to the pet store, paying for the mouse, taking the mouse home, building a home for it, getting in trouble with their parents, and then having to take the mouse back to the pet store — show how well she can create a simple story with an idea, a problem, and a solution. For her next story, I am going to introduce the idea of a sequel.

a cartoon is shared with a class, the creator can elaborate on particular parts or other students can ask questions to better understand the creator's thoughts and process. You can review the animations while using the Cartoon Event Checklist (form 8.3) to quickly gather, record, and assess a child's understanding of basic story events.

Using Multi-Touch Mobile Devices to Exhibit Learning

Not only do multi-touch mobile devices offer children many opportunities to create, but they also offer teachers and children a variety of ways to show what children have learned in a particular experience or over a series of experiences. Applications offer opportunities for parents and families to listen, watch, and interact with their child's progress and development. Teachers and children can use multi-touch mobile devices to

✓ share e-portfolios,

✓ showcase video books, and

✓ support next year's class.

SHARE E-PORTFOLIOS

E-portfolios are a useful way to electronically compile items to track and exhibit children's developmental progress. E-portfolios can be created and maintained using a computer, laptop, or multi-touch mobile devices. If you are using a laptop or computer, you will need to scan in work samples and import photographs. Multi-touch mobile devices provide the opportunity to gather, store, and share these items all in one device. E-portfolios allow teachers and other professionals to share

- audio recordings taken during conversations or conferences,

- video books published by child,

- audio recordings taken during learning experiences with a music teacher,

- videos taken during learning experiences,

- photographs of a child at work, and

- photographs of work samples.

Having these items available on a multi-touch mobile device provides an opportunity to conduct high-quality and meaningful conferences with parents. Sharing these items allows parents to see and hear their child's learning in action. They are given the opportunity to engage with authentic materials that help them leave a conference feeling informed and supported.

SHOWCASE VIDEO BOOKS

The strategies in this chapter include using iPad applications such as Draw for iPad, Drawing Pad, and SonicPics to foster the development of early writing skills. At an open house or curriculum night, a teacher can have a number of iPads out with children's video books loaded on them. This can provide families with knowledge about how the children are learning essential literacy skills while at the same time learning essential technology skills. As the families circulate through the iPads and view the video books, the children can describe the process of planning, creating, publishing, and sharing their video books.

SUPPORT NEXT YEAR'S CLASS

Over the course of a school year, children in early childhood classrooms learn a whole host of routines, social skills, and purposes for materials. Teachers can help next year's new class of children make the transition by enlisting the existing class to help create a video about the classroom. Children can work with you on an iPad2 to take video and snapshots of classroom events and spaces. You can take audio recordings of children describing the purposes for materials and routines. Then you can use the SonicPics or the iMovie applications to assemble the video.

After a full year of preschool children working with their sixth-grade learning partners, both classes teamed up to create a video for the following year's classes. This video provided some tips for the next year's learning partners. Creating this video provided the children with a meaningful and emotionally satisfying way to reflect on the year and what they had learned with their partners.

◆　◆　◆

Never before have doctors, business executives, therapists, field researchers, teachers, children, and families had a single device that can serve so many purposes, meet so many needs, and make communication, collaboration, and creation so easy. Multi-touch mobile devices bring the world to our fingertips through video, photographs, literature, games, music, e-mail, videoconferencing, audio files, and so much more. As an early childhood teacher, you are always searching for another tool to help support inquiry to foster fervent learning. The possibilities with this tool are endless.

» TOOLBOX TIPS

SEARCHING FOR HIGH-QUALITY APPLICATIONS

Finding high-quality applications can be difficult. Be sure to read any reviews given for applications when shopping in the iTunes App Store. There are some reliable websites that review applications that are helpful as well. Appolicious, www.appolicious.com, offers visitors the ability to search for applications, read reviews, and see tutorial and informational videos on particular applications. Other helpful websites with similar features include Moms with Apps, http://momswithapps.com; Common Sense Media, www.commonsensemedia.org; Technology in Special Education, http://techin-specialed.com. These resources are user interactive. Individuals may have opportunities to create profiles where they can share their top-rated applications, see other users' top-rated applications, pose questions, and hold conversations with others. Frameworks for teachers to review applications are described in chapter 9.

Forms 8

8.1 Digital Book Recording Assessment Checklist for Prereaders

www.redleafpress.org/tech/8-1.pdf

8.2 Digital Book Recording Assessment Checklist for Readers

www.redleafpress.org/tech/8-2.pdf

8.3 Cartoon Event Checklist

www.redleafpress.org/tech/8-3.pdf

8.1 Digital Book Recording Assessment Checklist for Prereaders

Child(ren):

Date:

Digital Book:

Skill:	Yes	No
Discusses author and illustrator roles		
Poses questions about text		
Makes observations from illustrations		
Begins to make inferences		
Makes text-to-self connections		
Makes text-to-text connections		
Poses predictions		

Notes for Future Learning Experiences:

8.2 Digital Book Recording Assessment Checklist for Readers

Child(ren):

Date:

Digital Book:

Skills:	Yes	No
Recognizes known letters		
Recognizes familiar sight words		
Makes text-to-world connections		
Discusses inferences using background knowledge and text		
Reflects on predictions		
Creates new predictions while continuing to read		
Employs comprehension strategies independently to understand text		
Discusses author's style of writing		

Notes for Future Learning Experiences:

8.3 Cartoon Event Checklist

Child(ren):

Date:

Cartoon Title:

Plot:	Yes	No
Basic plot for characters and setting		
Setting:		
Logical for chosen plot		
Consistent throughout story when necessary		
Changes throughout story when necessary		
Characters:		
Logical characters for chosen plot		
Logical characters for chosen setting		
Problem:		
Logical problem for chosen characters		
Logical problem for chosen setting		
Resolution:		
Logical resolution for chosen characters		
Logical resolution for chosen problem		

Notes for Future Learning Experiences:

9
Infusing Technology into the Classroom

www.redleafpress.org/tech/9-1.aspx

In chapter 1, Chip Donohue discussed the importance of teachers educating themselves about today's technology. He writes about how fast technology is moving and how early childhood teachers need to support young children in developing skills and awareness to incorporate this technology into the fabric of their lives. The strategies provided in the previous chapters were intended to help you do just that; to identify and understand developmentally appropriate practices at various levels and how they fit into a sequence of other experiences. The practices described in this book address a variety of disciplines and technologies. It is my hope that you apply the strategies in this book to fit your program or school, whether you are searching for additional strategies to implement with existing technology or for technology to enhance or develop a setting or classroom.

You may have read a book or been to a workshop or conference session that has energized, inspired, and refueled you. You finish the book or leave the workshop ready to go back into your classrooms to try out every new tool.

Too often, however, you are given amazing tools to use without information on how to use them appropriately. This chapter explores goal setting, curriculum mapping, technology-skill mapping, and ongoing reflection. It addresses using the goals you set to determine the technology you acquire. It also speaks to the importance of communicating and collaborating with administrators, fellow teachers, and families to support implementation. In addition, this chapter explores ways to identify and plan for the skills children must acquire to use certain technologies. After providing experiences to children, you need to reflect on their effectiveness. Therefore this chapter provides the evaluation tools to ensure that children's experiences with technology adhere to developmentally appropriate practice.

Acquiring Technology

Acquiring technology for educational use can be difficult. There are a variety of obstacles that programs and schools may encounter. Administrators are under an overwhelming amount of stress to drive student progress and growth through increased test scores. Some administrators search for the tool that will increase the score tomorrow rather than investing in tools that offer the potential for long-term academic success for children. Since technology tools come with a price tag and funding is a common obstacle in schools and programs, schools need to find creative ways to secure funding for technology. Obtaining support from school families and community members can also be an obstacle. When schools provide education and open dialogue with families and community members, telling them how technology carries out larger vision and goals for children, partnerships and support systems can be a powerful result.

WORKING WITH YOUR ADMINISTRATION

Tracey Conners, principal of Fair Park Elementary in West Bend, Wisconsin, knows the possibilities that technology can provide for her students. Here she identifies the iPad as a tool that can be used to support learners in all sorts of ways.

As a building administrator, every decision I make must be deeply rooted in the indicators of high-functioning organizations: visionary leadership, investment in high-quality, directed staff development, agility within the system, and value of innovation and efficacy. When the iPad was released in 2010, many felt the shift in our collective technological future. The ability of this multi-touch, interactive tool in the classroom was seemingly unlimited. However, the implementation of this new tool can be controversial and seen as a luxury and not an "essential need" in our public schools, especially in early childhood and lower elementary classrooms.

When I asked the district's technology administrator about acquiring iPads, he did not just write us a blank check. Instead, he asked the essential question that forced us to outline our clear purpose. "How will this tool help the West Bend School District and the students at Fair Park Elementary achieve its mission: To Prepare All Students for College Readiness and Career Success?"

Our goal in the content of reading was letter recognition, letter sounds, and sight words. In the content of math, number recognition, number sense and measurement, specifically money and telling of time. The teachers selected applications (apps) that focused on these specific skills and designed pre- and post-assessments that allowed us to measure student growth. The teachers were also interested in measuring how students felt about school, themselves as learners, and technology, so a pre- and post-assessment was developed for these areas as well.

In order to support the professional development of the teachers, I needed to make time in the day for these teachers to meet. They spent the time identifying apps, evaluating the potential effectiveness of the apps, and sharing ideas for using the iPads in classrooms. In addition, I was always on the lookout for ways to bring in nearby university presenters who focus on iPad technology in the classroom, as well as reading *Macworld* and numerous professional journals on the different ways to effectively utilize technology in the classroom.

The need to do more with less is a constant in almost all districts. The West Bend School district is the nineteenth largest in the state of Wisconsin and in contrast has the sixth-lowest spending in the state, so we do not have money to spend on a fad. We knew that if we were going to purchase iPads, we needed to have a clear plan for their use and a clear way to show their effectiveness. As the building administrator, I meet with our district's technology administrator to outline both our predicted costs as well as the plans for implementation, evaluation, and modeling the uses of the technologies.

The teachers at Tracey's school are using iPads in their classrooms because Tracey sees technology as another tool that her teachers can use to support the social-emotional and academic growth in their youngest learners. Tracey's teachers assessed the children's feelings about their abilities in math and reading. These assessments continue to play an important role in how the iPads are used. She also sees the value in providing professional development for her teachers. When teachers are not provided professional development, they may slide down a slippery slope into inappropriate and unreflective uses with technology. Tracey knows that technology is an investment in a child's success for today and tomorrow.

Teachers working in schools with administrators who do not necessarily yet share the same vision as Tracey can use the work of those who are using technology successfully as evidence that it can support growth and development. Action research within classrooms can be a powerful tool to convince the weary. Starting small, as described in chapter 1, can also be an important element to consider here. When Tracey first purchased iPads, she started with a few of them and has slowly begun to acquire more as she has noticed the students' success increase. This strategy is a smart one, because it lowers financial risk. Then, as success with the technology is observed, the investment can grow, or, if success is not evident, the use of the technology and the technology itself can be reviewed and a new course taken without a major financial loss.

SECURING FUNDING

As the economy continues to pull funding from school districts across the country, technology can be difficult to obtain. School districts have discovered the value of DonorsChoose, www.donorschoose.org. This website provides an amazing grant-writing resource for public school teachers. To write a grant, teachers answer a series of questions that address the intention behind the project and materials. Individuals at DonorsChoose review all grants before they are posted to the website. Once grants are available for public view, teachers can share an online link directly to their grant with families and area businesses. In the first session of a workshop series I led for the Chicago Public Schools, I discussed how DonorsChoose can support teachers in acquiring technology equipment for classrooms. Crystal Jones, a preschool teacher in the Roseland neighborhood on the far South Side of Chicago, who was feeling defeated and unmotivated, spoke with me afterward. She felt that she was not going to be able to implement much of anything over the course of the year because of a lack of support. As the year went on, Crystal's feelings changed.

> Brian's first class discussed technology in the classroom and funding sources; that's when Brian introduced DonorsChoose. Years prior, I had created a DonorsChoose account but had not mustered up enough faith that donors would fund projects in my community. So I never created a project. Now Brian told me that I should give it a try, that he knew many who were successful in getting projects funded. Brian's face was sincere and encouraging, so I did. I went home and immediately began to create a project for a convection oven for nutrition projects with my preschoolers; after all, I had borrowed one from a neighbor to complete my last

two cooking activities. The wait began! When no donations were submitted, I started to lose faith but remembered Brian's encouraging words, "It works." It was about this time that a community member saw my project online and gave the principal at my school a $25 DonorsChoose gift card for my use. I was amazed and mystified! After applying the gift card toward my grant project, I utilized the website tools to e-mail the grant request to friends. I also posted it on Facebook. Soon my brother and a friend of mine contributed an additional $25 each. I was astonished, and the wheels started turning. One week later, two additional donors contributed, which completed my project! It took only two months for this project to be funded. I was a new believer in DonorsChoose. I quickly created a second project, requesting materials to support fire safety instruction. This second project was funded in just six weeks! Once again, I was motivated to create a third project. I requested materials to replace our broken listening center, a new CD player, and headphones. This project was funded in only four weeks by the charity organization of our local baseball team, the Chicago White Sox. Now I know Brian was right; it does work. The most important realization from this experience is hope. With school budgets decreasing, I now know that I have the ability to acquire materials and supplies that I need to offer a quality education to my at-risk preschoolers. And that is priceless!

Crystal Jones, preschool teacher, reflects on how she's become more comfortable with the children in her class using the technology she recently acquired. (*www.redleafpress.org/tech /9-2.aspx*)

During one week in February, 6,144 people donated to 773 projects, reaching 43,767 children in the United States. I think teachers, particularly in urban areas, feel Crystal's original discouragement. When times get tough, it may seem like the easiest solution is to give up. In these times, remember Crystal's message to keep moving and keep hoping. Crystal now has an iPad 2 that she uses with the preschoolers she teaches. She is overjoyed with the progress she has made, the confidence she has developed, and the experiences she has been able to provide the preschoolers.

Nonprofit educational settings outside of the public sector can utilize Digital Wish, www.digitalwish.com. Just as at DonorsChoose, teachers can create a project that seeks necessary materials and equipment to carry out a particular experience. Donors can search by teacher, schools, or school district and contribute to those they choose.

SHARING THE IMPORTANCE OF TECHNOLOGY WITH FAMILIES

Families want to support their children and often rely on teachers for insight on how to do this. When families approach you with reluctance to use technology, they are simply wondering if it is the best way to support their child's growth and development. When you are confident in your practice and can clearly articulate how technology supports their children's growth and development, families are more likely to develop comfort and support for the technology's presence in the classroom. It is important to provide families with orientation sessions that help them get acquainted with the uses and operations of classroom technologies. When these sessions are done effectively, children and families can discuss school experiences with a shared understanding of how and why certain experiences were carried out. Moreover, families can develop firmer understandings of the technology use in schools when they are invited in at the implementation process. Arlyn Chin, a parent of two elementary-age boys, writes here about her journey—one that is similar to that of many parents today.

> Not too long ago, it seemed to me that parents highly discouraged their young children from using technology. As recently as eight years ago, when my first child was born, I heard other parents warning me that overexposing my child to a computer, video games, or even a cell phone would hinder his ability to think for himself. It seemed like many of my friends and family felt that the use of technical devices would force children to rely on technology and not their brains. I totally bought into it.
>
> It wasn't until Jackson was about five that I started to allow him to play with my smartphone and with video games. It started out (as in

many of my friends' cases) as providing a distraction when we were in public, like a restaurant or a coffee shop. Soon Jackson began to ask more and more to "play with Mommy's phone," and I started letting him have more technology time. The decision was a tough one and was mostly initiated by the fact that I didn't want him to be the only child who didn't know how to use a computer or play a video game. Like many children exposed to technology, he caught on quickly. Soon his younger brother, Col, followed suit, and before I knew it, both my sons knew how to maneuver around our computer, my iPhone, and the family iPad. My husband and I decided to harness their newfound love of technology and steer them to educational applications and age-appropriate games.

What I discovered (and hadn't thought about previously) was that allowing my sons to learn on a platform that was interesting to them made learning exciting for them. Their curiosity was piqued, and it helped augment their budding confidence when it came to reading, writing, and general learning. Using technology made learning fun, and it seeped into their everyday lives. Reading a book became a lot more fun when they had built a confidence in reading via reading- and writing-based applications on our iPad. They became excited when they could spew out facts that they learned on applications like BrainPOP. They felt smart and wanted to learn more. The introduction of technology at home, coupled with appropriate parental monitoring, gave my sons the additional desire to learn on their own and feel confident that they could maneuver through a technology device.

Within the last couple of years, I have found that the use of technology in school is becoming more accessible to my children. I will be the first to admit that I didn't put a lot of confidence in my children to actually use technology in school for learning purposes. I was thrilled when iPads were launched at their elementary school but thought that they would really just be using them to spell words and paint pretty pictures. I was wrong. I was completely astonished when I learned that my first grader was learning how to research dinosaurs, take notes, and present his findings on an iPad. I was floored when my children started coming home, marching straight to our home Mac, launching applications, and using them to share ideas. They wanted to do research on their own and wanted to show Mommy and Daddy how to do it, using technology. They wanted to share what they were learning in school and how proficient they were becoming on each of the devices. They were learning and spewing out gobs of information from time in their technology classes.

I have had numerous opportunities to volunteer in both my sons' classrooms while the children were using various technology devices. What I found, in addition to the fact that children genuinely love working with technology, was that the technology made it more efficient to pass and share information. Gone were the stacks of papers that were needed to collect thoughts, and what took their place was a hard drive with voice clips and iPads filled with the children's research. In classrooms where student population continues to grow, technology made organizing information more efficient and, in some cases, allowed parents to view their children's work at home. I even heard comments from parents who weren't able to volunteer that they felt involved in their child's learning because they could watch a video clip or hear a sound bite that their child created. It brought them closer to the classroom.

My sons are one grade apart from each other in school and are entering their third year of using technology in their classrooms. My observation has been that each grade has introduced technology components at the appropriate time. In kindergarten, my sons were learning the various uses for technology (e.g., video recording, picture taking, voice recording). In first grade, my sons were introduced to the use of technology to do research and organize their thoughts. In second grade, my son is learning that technology can be used to complete entire projects. He's learning that after doing research and organization, he can merge various pieces into a collective project. He is starting to identify specific applications by their function and how the applications relate to building a project. I have been pleased with the way technology has been introduced at grade-specific levels within their school.

The challenge I've observed has been how to maintain the momentum between school and home. For our family, it's been a seamless transition, since we own many of the devices the school uses. I'm sure not all families can say the same. The students are lucky that they have access to technology at school, but the challenge has been reinforcing at home what is learned in school. Many parents are not technologically savvy and struggle with understanding what their children are learning. In addition, many parents own the same devices but don't know how to keep continuity between school and home.

One way that my family keeps abreast of what is being taught technically is by subscribing to the school technology department's podcasts and RSS feeds. If I were to ask other parents if they do the same, chances are, they probably don't even know these communication tools exist. Although the sharing mechanisms are in place, communicating that they even exist doesn't often happen. Recently, a parent approached me about a blog he started for specifically sharing information about technology at the school with other families. He felt that parents didn't have an outlet to ask questions about the various applications and devices being used at the school, and he hopes his blog alleviates that problem and provides a common place for discussion.

There are many ways that families can support the use of technology at school. Aside from advocating the use of technology at home, they can encourage their children to join after-school programs and/or ask them to share what they learned in technology class at home. Schools are oftentimes tight on resources, so families could pool together to help share ideas and their own personal technical knowledge with one another. A blog or a mailing list is a great start.

In addition to nontechnological volunteer time, I have assisted teachers with recording children on computers and iPads and have used various devices to help the technology department capture data for their program. I have made movies to capture memories for the children. The list sometimes seems endless. The reason I have been so involved with the school and the classroom is precisely to help augment the use of technology within the school.

Arlyn found a niche at her children's school where she feels she can contribute to the whole school. Having provided support to the teachers in carrying out experiences, she helped the students in classrooms engage with technology in ways that truly supported the goals of the teachers. A partnership is clearly evident between her and the school—one that provides a great example of the importance of including families in your technology efforts.

Beth Lambert, first-grade teacher, describes using technology to exhibit learning and development during parent-teacher conferences. (*www.redleafpress.org/tech/9-3.aspx*)

Technology Skill Mapping

After confronting the common challenges teachers face and exploring options to overcome them, you should consider goals that will help move children forward with the experiences you want to provide. Chapter 1 discussed curriculum mapping. This is one way to identify a scope and sequence for the disciplines you teach so you have a vision and intended path in mind. Regardless of the method you use, having that map in place will make it easier to connect learning with the use of technology.

After developing a curriculum map for a given discipline and plugging in strategies for implementing technology, you need to develop a technology-skill map to determine when and how children will learn particular skills they need to successfully engage with the technology throughout the year.

For example, a kindergarten teacher wants his students to further develop their ability to retell stories. After completing the Classroom Equipment Survey (form 1.3), he identifies two iPads in a location in his room where children can use them independently or in pairs. He also has the necessary equipment to charge the iPads when needed. After completing the Assessing Your Skills Sheet (form 1.4), he becomes confident enough with navigating an iPad to use it in the classroom in the next few weeks. While gathering resources for an upcoming author study, he discovers a digital book iPad application for Marc Brown's *Arthur Writes a Story* (ScrollMotion 2011). The application has the option to record up to ten recordings of the story. The teacher decides that this would

9.1 Technology Skill Map

GRADE LEVEL: Kindergarten   DISCIPLINE/CONTENT AREA: Social Studies/Families

MONTH	TECHNOLOGY	TECHNOLOGY SKILL	ACTIVITY
September	Multi-touch mobile device	Swipe, scroll, find and open Photos application.	View photographs of children in class.
October	Document camera and multi-touch mobile device	Knowledge of uses of a document camera and how it works with a computer and a projector.	View photographs of children's families projected onto screen
November	Multi-touch mobile device	Knowledge of the many uses for a multi-touch mobile device How to take turns with a multi-touch mobile device while in a small group Understand how to start and stop a video in an application	In small groups, view videos of children celebrating holidays and events in different cultures.
December	Webcam	Awareness that people can communicate in many ways including video conferencing with programs such as Skype and FaceTime Individuals video-conferencing need to be able to see themselves on their screen in order for their receiver to see them	Video conference with a classmate who is visiting family out of town
January	Interactive whiteboard	Awareness that interactive whiteboards can be used to explore websites without having to be at a computer. Interactive whiteboards become a large touch screen to navigate a website	An expert of Chinese culture visits and uses an interactive whiteboard to view the website www.topmarks.co.uk/chinesenewyear/DragonDance.aspx to learn about the Dragon Dance.

be an opportunity for his students to record themselves retelling the story and then listening to their own reading to check for accuracy and rerecording if necessary. After filling out the Planning for Student Equipment Use Sheet (form 1.2), he determines that the children are familiar with swiping and scrolling on an iPad, because they have used iPads in the classroom before. They have not, however, used a digital book. To prepare his students for upcoming experiences with digital books, the teacher determines that he will need to develop experiences that address the following concepts: the difference between a printed and a digital book, how a digital book is similar to and different from other applications they have used already, and how to record a reading in the application. Using the Technology Skill Map (form 9.1), he can identify technology skills the children need to engage in learning activities. In doing so, he is ensuring that his students are fully prepared to engage with the iPad and application. The Technology Skill Map can help teachers collect all the technology strategies children will engage in over the course of the year and identify a sequence of experiences to develop skills necessary to participate in later experiences.

Earlier, I advised teachers to collaborate through the planning and mapping process. It is equally important to come together to reflect on strategies tried. When teachers come together to discuss and reflect, they can look at experiences through a variety of lenses and perspectives. Chapter 7 discusses how the Recorded Learning Experience Reflection Sheet (form 7.1) can help teachers reflect on learning experiences. It is important to remember that reflection is not always a solitary task. When teachers cluster around a video of a group of children engaged in an activity, there are six, eight, even ten eyes and ears observing the video. Each teacher will notice different skills being exhibited and will pose different questions. Collaboration and discussion are powerful and essential tools for teachers to use in refining practices and supporting the children in their classroom.

Evaluating Strategies and Applications for Developmental Appropriateness and Effectiveness

When teachers have a clear picture of the curriculum they are teaching and what technological skills children need to engage with various technologies, teachers can critically reflect on the experiences that have been carried out. Throughout this book, I have provided interactive forms to help guide your reflection and assessment. The form shown here is from Harry Walker's Application Evaluation Rubric. It was developed to evaluate iPod and iPad applications. When Harry Walker of Johns Hopkins University noticed applications starting to be used in schools, he quickly recognized a need for an evaluative

Domain	1	2	3	4
		Evaluation Rubric for IPod Apps		
Curriculum Connection	Skill(s) reinforced in the app are not clearly connected to the targeted skill or concept	Skill(s) reinforced are prerequisite or foundation skills for the targeted skill or concept	Skill(s) reinforced are related to the targeted skill or concept	Skill(s) reinforced are strongly connected to the targeted skill or concept
Authenticity	Skills are practiced in a rote or isolated fashion (e.g., flashcards)	Skills are practiced in a contrived game/simulation format	Some aspects of the app are presented an authentic learning environment	Targeted skills are practiced in an authentic format/problem-based learning environment
Feedback	Feedback is limited to correctness of student responses	Feedback is limited to correctness of student responses and may allow for student to try again	Feedback is specific and results in improved student performance (may include tutorial aids)	Feedback is specific and results in improved student performance; Data is available electronically to student and teacher
Differentiation	App offers no flexibility (settings cannot be altered)	App offers limited flexibility (e.g., few levels such as easy, medium, hard)	App offers more than one degree of flexibility to adjust settings to meet student needs	App offers complete flexibility to alter settings to meet student needs
User Friendliness	Students need constant teacher supervision in order to use the app	Students need to have the teacher review how to the use the app on more than one occasion	Students need to have the teacher review how to the use the app	Students can launch and navigate within the app independently
Student Motivation	Students avoid the use of the app or complain when the app is assigned by the teacher	Students view the app as "more schoolwork" and may be off-task when directed by the teacher to use the app	Students will use the app as directed by the teacher	Students are highly motivated to use the app and select it as their first choice from a selection of related choices of apps

Created by Harry Walker – Johns Hopkins University   10/18/2010
Please contact for permission to use hwalker@bcps.org

tool, so he gathered what he knows is important for learning and compiled it into a framework for educators. He includes six essential domains teachers should consider when critically reviewing applications: curriculum connection, authenticity, feedback, differentiation, user friendliness, and motivation. These domains, described in detail in the divisions of the rubric, provide teachers with opportunities to consider what is and what could be present in an application. These domains help teachers determine to what extent the applications address learning standards and curriculum goals. Too often, teachers use technology for the "wow factor" and not necessarily for the curriculum connection. Harry's domains provide teachers with an opportunity to consider the amount of engagement and interactivity between the device and the child.

Kathy Schrock (http://kathyschrock.net, kathy@kathyschrock.net) discovered Harry's evaluation rubric and adapted it to meet the needs of her evaluative practices for working with young children. As Kathy developed her

---

9.2 Critical Evaluation of an iPad/iPod App

Name: **Brad Kleinman, Librarian** Date: **3/12/2012**

What is the title of the app? **I Spy Riddle Race** Cost: **$.99**

Creator of the app **Scholastic, Inc.** iTunes URL:
http://itunes.apple.com/us/app/i-spy-riddle-race/id329373688?mt=8

Content area(s): **Reading, Language, and Science** Grade level: **Ages: 4 - 8**

CONTENT AND COMPONENTS OF THE APP	Yes	No
Curriculum connection: Are the skills reinforced connected to targeted skill/concept?	X	
Authenticity: Are skills practiced in an authentic format/problem-based environment?	X	
Feedback: Is feedback specific and result in improved student performance?	X	
Differentiation: Does the app offer flexibility to alter settings to meet student needs?	X	
User friendliness: Can students can launch and navigate within the app independently?	X	
Student motivation: Are students motivated to use the app and select it to use often?	X	
Reporting: Is assessment/summary data available electronically to the student/teacher?	X	
Sound: Does the music/sound in the app add to the educational aspects of the content?	X	
Instructions: Are the instructions included within the app helpful to the student?	X	
Support page: Does the app's supporting web page provide additional useful information?	X	

SUMMARY OF THE APP
Using the data you have collected above, explain why you would or would not recommend this application for use in the classroom. Include any specific ideas you have for its use.

This applications can be used in all sorts of ways. This application provides another way for children to engage with the I Spy book series, perfect for an author study of Jean Marzollo and Walter Wick. The application is interactive as it requires children to move the iPad in certain ways to move marbles to the appropriate place. Children have the ability to zoom in on the screen to take a close look at the pictures to search for the given list of items to find. This application also has a time clock so teachers know how long a child has been working with a certain page. There is also an individual in the application who provides directions orally on how to operate each part of the application.

From "Critical Evaluation of an iPad/iPod App" by Kathy Schrock, © 2011. Adapted from "Evaluation Rubric for iPad/iPod Apps" by Harry Walker. Johns Hopkins University, 2010. Reprinted with permission.

9.3 Evaluating Strategy Effectiveness Sheet

Lesson Objective:
Children will observe photographs of families of the children in their class.

Task/Activity:
In small groups, children will use a multi-touch mobile device to observe photos of families.

Is the strategy supported by the NAEYC Position Statement, 2012	Yes X	No

Evidence of support:
Children are provided with experiences to learn about how technology can be used to learn about our community.

Were the objectives achieved?	Yes X	No

Yes	No
How do you know? The children were engaged as they pointed out people they knew. They leaned over and observed other children's devices as children saw exciting photographs. After observing the photographs, many children continued talking and asking questions to each other about what they saw.	How do you know?
Will you use this strategy again? Yes	Can this strategy be used differently to meet the objectives?

Yes	No	Yes	No
How? I will use this strategy to show photographs of different types of homes as we move forward with our study of families.	Why?	How?	How will you reteach?

Critical Evaluation Rubric (form 9.2) (http://school.discoveryeducation.com/schrockguide/pdf/evalipad.pdf), she made sure to keep the essential pieces of the rubric but condensed it for easy review. In my work with young children and applications, I, too, created an evaluative tool that met my needs. I have used the Evaluating Strategy Effectiveness Sheet (form 9.3) to quickly determine if a strategy has been effective and whether I need to revisit certain concepts with additional activities. The Evaluating Strategy Effectiveness Sheet encourages you to consider the NAEYC position statement on technology. This statement provides recommendations for various age levels. You can review these levels to determine where your strategy fits into the recommendations and to see if your strategy is in fact developmentally appropriate.

As various devices and strategies are invented and developed, implementation models specific to them may be developed. Friend and colleague Warren Buckleitner (2011b) created an eight-step plan to set up a multi-touch preschool classroom. In his plan, he succinctly provides important information about budget, number of iPads, necessary accessories, centers, and activities in which to include them, high-quality applications for the iPads, and organization and security measures to consider. Warren has knowledge and experience using iPads with teaching children, so his offerings to the early childhood community are extremely meaningful.

We need to keep the conversations about technology in early childhood classrooms going. As these conversations move forward, and as teachers try new things, new models and strategies will be developed. When these strategies are shared, teachers and children benefit. With today's technology, our means of communicating have expanded. With today's social media possibilities, teachers can learn about new strategies with a couple of clicks, swipes, and scrolls.

I hope this book has helped you better understand what developmentally appropriate practices with technology should look like, feel like, and sound like. I hope you feel that you can confidently use this resource to find a starting place in your own setting, whether you have a single digital camera or a classroom set of iPads.

Today's technology puts a multitude of possibilities in the hands of children. They can share their ideas and learning with children in their class or with families and relatives across the globe over a webcam. They can publish a book and develop confident identities as authors or illustrators. They have the opportunity to try on the roles of community members by recording and sharing commercials, announcements, and radio shows. Children today have the entire world at their fingertips. By using technology as part of the curriculum, children can develop a solid sense of inquiry and the high-level thinking skills necessary to propel our society into what's to come—who knows what that will be?

With today's technology, educators, administrators, and families have the opportunity to empower children to ask questions, create, communicate, learn, wonder, and invest in lifelong learning.

Forms

9

9.1 Technology Skill Map

www.redleafpress.org/tech/9-1.pdf

9.2 Kathy Schrock's Critical Evaluation Rubric

www.redleafpress.org/tech/9-2.pdf

9.3 Evaluating Strategy Effectiveness Sheet

www.redleafpress.org/tech/9-3.pdf

9.1 Technology Skill Map

GRADE LEVEL: _____ DISCIPLINE/CONTENT AREA: _____

MONTH	TECHNOLOGY	TECHNOLOGY SKILL	ACTIVITY
September			
October			
November			
December			
January			

9.1 Technology Skill Map

GRADE LEVEL: _____ DISCIPLINE/CONTENT AREA: _____

MONTH	TECHNOLOGY	TECHNOLOGY SKILL	ACTIVITY
February			
March			
April			
May			
June			

9.2 Critical Evaluation of an iPad/iPod App

Name:		Date:
What is the title of the app?		Cost:
Creator of the app	iTunes URL:	
Content area(s):		Grade level:

CONTENT AND COMPONENTS OF THE APP	Yes	No
Curriculum connection: Are the skills reinforced connected to targeted skill/concept?		
Authenticity: Are skills practiced in an authentic format/problem-based environment?		
Feedback: Is feedback specific and result in improved student performance?		
Differentiation: Does the app offer flexibility to alter settings to meet student needs?		
User friendliness: Can students can launch and navigate within the app independently?		
Student motivation: Are students motivated to use the app and select it to use often?		
Reporting: Is assessment/summary data available electronically to the student/teacher?		
Sound: Does the music/sound in the app add to the educational aspects of the content?		
Instructions: Are the instructions included within the app helpful to the student?		
Support page: Does the app's supporting web page provide additional useful information?		

SUMMARY OF THE APP

Using the data you have collected above, explain why you would or would not recommend this application for use in the classroom. Include any specific ideas you have for its use.

From "Critical Evaluation of an iPad/iPod App" by Kathy Schrock, © 2011. Adapted from "Evaluation Rubric for iPad/iPod Apps" by Harry Walker. Johns Hopkins University, 2010. Reprinted with permission.

9.3 Evaluating Strategy Effectiveness Sheet

Lesson Objective:		

Task/Activity:		

Is the strategy supported by the NAEYC Position Statement, 2012	Yes	No

Evidence of support:

Were the objectives achieved?	Yes	No

Yes	No
How do you know?	How do you know?
Will you use this strategy again?	Can this strategy be used differently to meet the objectives?

Yes	No	Yes	No
How?	Why?	How?	How will you reteach?

References

American Academy of Pediatrics. 2011. "Media Use by Children Younger Than 2 Years." doi:10.1542/peds.2011–1753.

Barron, Brigid, Gabrielle Cayton-Hodges, Laura Bofferding, Carol Copple, Linda Darling-Hammond, and Michael H. Levine. 2011. *Take a Giant Step: A Blueprint for Teaching Young Children in a Digital Age*. New York: The Joan Ganz Cooney Center at Sesame Workshop. www.joanganzcooneycenter.org/upload_kits/jgcc_takeagiantstep.pdf.

Buckleitner, Warren. 2011a. "Moving beyond the Debate on Technology and Young Children." Webinar presented through Early Childhood Investigations, June 1.

———. 2011b. "Setting Up a Multi-Touch Preschool: An Eight-Step Plan, with Costs, Apps, and Other Details." *Children's Technology Review* 19 (132): 5–9.

Chiong, Cynthia, and Carly Shuler. 2010. *Learning: Is There an App for That? Investigations of Young Children's Usage and Learning with Mobile Devices and Apps*. New York: The Joan Ganz Cooney Center at Sesame Workshop. www.joanganzcooneycenter.org/upload_kits/learningapps_final_110140.pdf.

Clemens, Arine, Traci Moore, and Brian Nelson. 2001. "Math Intervention 'SMART' Project (Student Mathematical Analysis and Reasoning with Technology)." http://downloads.smarttech.com/media/sitecore/en/pdf/research_library/math/math_intervention_smart_project%20_student_mathematical_analysis_and_reasoning_with_technology.pdf.

Copley, Juanita V. 2000. *The Young Child and Mathematics*. Washington, DC: National Association for the Education of Young Children.

Copple, Carol, and Sue Bredekamp. 2009. *Developmentally Appropriate Practice in Early Childhood Programs Serving Children from Birth through Age 8*. 3rd ed. Washington, DC: National Association for the Education of Young Children.

Couse, Leslie J., and Dora W. Chen. 2010. "A Tablet Computer for Young Children? Exploring Its Viability for Early Childhood Education." *Journal of Research on Technology in Education* 43 (1): 75–98.

Denton, Paula. 2007. *The Power of Our Words: The Teacher Language That Helps Children Learn*. Turners Falls, MA: Northeast Foundation for Children.

Greaves, Thomas, J. Hayes, L. Wilson, M. Gielniak, and R. Peterson. 2010. *The Technology Factor: Nine Keys to Student Achievement and Cost-Effectiveness*. Project RED and Pearson Education. www.pearsonfoundation.org/downloads/ProjectRED_TheTechnolgyFactor.pdf.

Harvey, Stephanie, and Anne Goudvis. 2007. *Strategies That Work: Teaching Comprehension for Understanding and Engagement*. 2nd ed. Portland, ME: Stenhouse.

Harvey, Stephanie, and Harvey Daniels. 2009. *Comprehension and Collaboration: Inquiry Circles in Action*. Portsmouth, NH: Heinemann.

Johnston, Peter. 2004. *Choice Words: How Our Language Affects Children's Learning*. Portland, ME: Stenhouse.

Millman, Joyce. 1999. "Fred Rogers." Salon.com. www.salon.com/1999/08/10/rogers_2.

Mitchell, Linda M. 2007. "Using Technology in Reggio Emilia-Inspired Programs." *Theory into Practice* 46 (1): 32–39.

NAEYC and FRC (National Association for the Education of Young Children and the Fred Rogers Center for Early Learning and Children's Media at Saint Vincent College). 2012. *Technology and Interactive Media as Tools in Early Childhood Programs Serving Children from Birth through Age 8.* Position statement. www.naeyc.org/files/naeyc/file/positions /PS_technology_WEB2.pdf.

Parette, Howard P., Jack J. Hourcade, Nichole M. Boeckmann, and Craig Blum. 2008. "Using Microsoft PowerPoint to Support Emergent Literacy Skill Development for Young Children At-Risk or Who Have Disabilities." *Early Childhood Education Journal* 36 (3): 233–39.

Parette Howard P., Amanda C. Quesenberry, and Craig Blum. 2010. "Missing the Boat with Technology Usage in Early Childhood Settings: A 21st Century View of Developmentally Appropriate Practice." *Early Childhood Education Journal* 37 (5): 335–43.

Plowman, Lydia, Joanna McPake, and Christine Stephen. 2008. "Just Picking It Up? Young Children Learning with Technology at Home." *Cambridge Journal of Education* 38 (3): 303–19.

Preston, Chris, and Lee Mowbray. 2008. "Use of SMART Boards for Teaching, Learning, and Assessment in Kindergarten Science." *Teaching Science* 54 (2): 50–53.

Rideout, Victoria J., and Elizabeth Hamel. 2006. *The Media Family: Electronic Media in the Lives of Infants, Toddlers, Preschoolers and Their Parents.* Menlo Park, CA: Henry J. Kaiser Family Foundation.

Riley, Dave, Robert R. San Juan, Joan Klinkner, and Ann Ramminger. 2007. *Social and Emotional Development: Connecting Science and Practice in Early Childhood Settings.* St. Paul, MN: Redleaf Press.

Roskos, Kathleen, Jeremy Brueck, and Sarah Widman. 2009. "Investigating Analytic Tools for e-Book Design in Early Literacy Learning." *Journal of Interactive Online Learning* 8 (3): 218–40.

Shuler, Carly. 2009. *Pockets of Potential: Using Mobile Technologies to Promote Children's Learning.* New York: The Joan Ganz Cooney Center at Sesame Workshop.

Stephen, Christine, and Lydia Plowman. 2008. "Enhancing Learning with Information and Communication Technologies in Pre-School." *Early Child Development and Care* 178 (6): 637–54.

Takeuchi, Lori M. 2011. *Families Matter: Designing Media for a Digital Age.* New York: The Joan Ganz Cooney Center at Sesame Workshop. www.joanganzcooneycenter.org/upload _kits/jgcc_familiesmatter.pdf.

Wang, Feng, Mable B. Kinzie, Patrick McGuire, and Edward Pan. 2010. "Applying Technology to Inquiry-Based Learning in Early Childhood Education." *Early Childhood Education Journal* 37 (5): 381–89.

Wellings, Jeanne, and Michael H. Levine. 2009. *The Digital Promise: Transforming Learning with Innovative Uses of Technology.* New York: The Joan Ganz Cooney Center at Sesame Workshop.

Woolfolk, Anita. 2004. *Educational Psychology.* 9th ed. Boston, MA: Pearson.

Yarosz, Donald J. 2007. "Integrating Interactive Theater Systems into Preschool Play Areas." *Futures Research Quarterly* 23 (3): 33–38.

Index

Image and Photography Credits

Photograph on page xxvi by Steve Wewerka

Images on page 1 courtesy of Elle Beehler and Kendall Everson

Photograph on page 40 courtesy of Maria Larios

Photographs on page 41 courtesy of Meghan Residori

Image of *Leer Sienta Bien* on page 45 courtesy of Serres

Photographs on pages 73, 103, and 176 courtesy of Kari Calabresa

Photographs on pages 75 and 144 (bottom) courtesy of Katie Blochowiak

Image of *The Letter Jj* on page 77 courtesy of Capstone Press

Photographs on page 101 courtesy of Sheri Burkeen

Photographs on pages 94 and 106 courtesy of Erin Stanfill

Photographs on page 145 courtesy of Kira Hamann

Photograph on page 164 courtesy of April Truttschel

Photograph of the author on the back cover courtesy of Emily Puerling

The remaining photographs and images (except on page 118) are courtesy of the author